JÄGERSTÄTTER

A PLAY BY FELIX MITTERER

UNO Press, University of New Orleans, LA 138, 2000 Lakeshore Drive. New Orleans, LA, 70148, USA. www.unopress.org.

This is a copublication of UNO Press and Center Austria. For more information, address www.centeraustria.org.

Printed in the United States of America

Cover and book design by Alex Dimeff

Cover and interior photos courtesy of Dr. Erna Putz

This project is made possible by a generous grant from The Dietrich W. Botstiber Foundation

www.botstiber.org

JÄGERSTÄTTER

A Play by Felix Mitterer

Translated by Gregor Thuswaldner with Robert Dassanowsky
Introduction by Gregor Thuswaldner
Preface by Günter Bischof

STUDIES IN CENTRAL EUROPEAN HISTORY CULTURE & LITERATURE

Center Austria

UNO PRESS

PREFACE

Günter Bischof

On August 9, 1943, the Nazis executed the Austrian conscientious objector Franz Jägerstätter in the prison in Brandenburg an der Havel (close to Berlin). The simple Upper Austrian farmer from Sankt Radegund from the Innviertel (close to Hitler's hometown of Braunau) was drafted for military service into the Wehrmacht in 1940. After weeks of basic training he was exempted from military service due to being "indispensable" on his farm. When he was drafted again in February 1943, the father of four young girls, Jägerstätter refused to serve due to his religious convictions. The following is the summary of his own defense from July 6, 1943 from the trial records of the Reich Military Court in Berlin:

> "Only in the past year had he become convinced that as a devout Catholic he was unable to engage in active military service. It was impossible for him to be a Catholic and at the same time a National Socialist. When he complied with the earlier conscription order, he did so because at that time he considered it a sin not to obey state orders. Now, however, God had given him the thought that it was not a sin to refuse armed service. There were matters in which one was obliged to obey God more than man; the commandment 'Thou shalt love they neighbor as thyself'

forbade him to engage in armed service, though he was prepared to serve as a paramedic."[1]

On November 1, 1943, only a few months after Jägerstätter's execution, the Allied foreign ministers gathered in Moscow and among many other decisions for the postwar world, also published a basic declaration on Austria. In it the British, Americans and Soviets agreed that Austria was "the first free country to fall victim to Hitlerite aggression" and therefore "shall be liberated from German domination." They announced that the imposed Austria's "annexation" by Germany on March 15, 1938, was "null and void" and therefore they wished to "reestablish an independent Austria." In a stern reminder the three Allies, however, told Austria that "she has a responsibility which she cannot evade for participation in the war on the side of Hitlerite Germany, and that in the final settlement account inevitably be taken of her own contribution to her liberation." In other words, the "Moscow Declaration" was a general call for Austrian resistance against the Nazis.[2]

---

1   A copy of the field judgement of the Reich Military Court, 2nd Senate, July 6, 1943, is in the Dokumentationsarchiv des Österreichischen Widerstandes file # 22057, it is quoted in Wolfgand Neugebauer, The Austrian Resistance 1938-1945, trans. John Nicolson and Eric Canepa (Vienna: Edition Steinbauer, 2014), p. 138 (a cameo sketch of Jägerstätter's life, ibid.136-138).

2   The English text of the Moscow Declaration is reprinted as Document 1 in the massive study by Gerald Stourzh, Um Einheit und Freiheit: Staatsvertrag, Neutralität und das Ende der Ost-West-Besetzung Österreichs 1945-1955 (4th ed. Vienna: Böhlau, 1998), p. 607. The most recent scholary study of interpretations of this key document is Stefan Karner/Alexander O. Tschubarjan, eds., Die Moskauer Deklaration 1943: "Österreich wieder herstellen" (Vienna: Böhlau, 2015).

Franz Jägerstätter's courageous refusal to serve in the German Wehrmacht was one of the most prominent acts of resistance by an ordinary Austrian during World War II. Not only that, Jägerstätter denounced Wehrmacht war crimes on the Eastern front long before anyone publically dared to utter a critique of what became known as the Holocaust. Jägerstätter thus gives the lie to all those Austrians who claimed not to have known about Nazi war crimes after the war. Yet in a strange twist of irony Jägerstätter's courageous acts of defiance of the Nazi regime were not prominently included in the record of the Austrian resistance movement(s) against Hitler and the Nazis for a long time in postwar Austrian historiography. While the reestablished Austrian government desperately was searching for every scrap of paper to build such an Austrian record of resistance against the Nazis to please the victorious Allies who were now Austria's occupiers. On April 27, 1945, the Provisional Renner Government incorporated the text of the Moscow Declaration of November 1, 1943, in its "Declaration of Independence" hook, line and sinker. Thus was born the state doctrine of Austria as victim of the Nazi regime (the "victims myth").

Soon after the rebirth the Austrian Republic, officials in the Foreign Ministry studiously began to collect the complete record of acts of Austrian resistance known at the time and published it in the *Red-White-Red Book* in 1946, just in time for the beginning of the negotiations for an Austrian peace treaty ("state treaty"). Plans for a second volume on the Austrian resistance were scrapped due to a lack of further evidence of resistance. Strangely, the inspiring story of Franz Jägerstätter was not incorporated in the *Red-White-Red Book Justice for Austria*.[3] Maybe, because the former Austrian Nazis began their slow comeback into the affairs of state and considered Jägerstätter a traitor rather than one of the most prominent Catholic resisters. Similarly, Jägerstätter's wife Franziska, who had encouraged him to follow his conscience during the war, experienced hostility and alienation from her neighbors and did not receive a war widow's pension from the Austrian government, while hundreds of thousands of widows of Wehrmacht soldiers, who had died on the battlefields of Europe, did receive such pensions. In a strange twist, in postwar Austrian mainstream public opinion soldiers who did "their duty" in the Wehrmacht (now also considered a murderous Nazi organization) were remembered as heroes, while resistance fighters were often pooh-poohed as "draft dodgers" and "traitors."

If one follows the historiography on the Austrian resistance after the war, Jägerstätter's defiance of the Nazi war machine was hardly mentioned. In 1958 Otto Molden, who had been in the O5 resistance group in the final months of the war, stressed the record of Catholic conservative and monarchist resistance groups, along with the deeds

---

3   The German version was Rot-Weiss-Rot-Buch: Darstellungenr, Dokumente und Nachweise zur Vorgeschichte und Geschichte der Okkupation Österreichs (nach amtlichen Quellen), Part One (Vienna , 1946); See also Neugebauer, Austrian Resistance, 15.

of his daredevil brother Fritz Molden in O5, but ignored the Communist resistance.[4] When the "Documentation Archives of the Austrian Resistance" (situated on the Left of the Austrian political spectrum) began its work in 1963, the Catholic Jägerstätter did not get a special mention or pride of place. Instead the broad resistance by Austrian communists, conservatives, monarchists, Catholics and the military resistance were studiously recorded. At the same time the Austrian government began financing a series of studies that concentrated on the Austrian resistance. Jägerstätter was barely mentioned.[5] The lonely voice of the American sociologist Gordon Zahn brought Jägerstätter back to the world's attention. Zahn stressed Jägerstätter's record as a conscientious objector and heaved him out of obscurity, at least in the Anglo-American world.[6]

When the American historian Radomir Luža published his history of the Austrian resistance in the 1980s, profiting from the rich research of the *Dokumentationsarchiv*, he stressed the record of the Communist resistance and ignored Jägerstätter again.[7] Only with the Catholic Church hierarchy in Austria taking interest in the record of the

4   Otto Molden, Der Ruf des Gewissens: Der österreichische Freiheitskampf 1938-1945 (Vienna-Munich, 1958).

5   Maria Szecsi/Karl Stadler, Die NS-Justiz in Östereich und ihre Opfer (Vienna-Munich, 1962).

6   Gordon Zahn, In Solitary Witness: The Life and Death of Franz Jägerstätter (Springfield, Il: Templegate, 1984); German translation: Er folgte seinem Gewissen: Das einsame Zeugnis des Franz Jägerstätter (Graz: Styria, 1967).

7   Radomir Luža, The Resistance in Austria 1938-1945 (Minneapolis: University of Minnesota Press, 1984).

Catholic resisters during World War II again, did they re-discover Jägerstätter. Maybe church leaders acted on their bad conscience, finally recognizing the Catholic Church hierarchy's craven submission to the Nazi regime during the war. On October 26, 2007, the Vatican through the bishop of Linz, beatified Jägerstätter. At last, the Catholic Church placed the halo of martyrdom on Jägerstätter. His predecessor as bishop of Linz during World War II had tried to talk Jägerstätter out of sacrificing his life for his faith and arrange himself with the Nazis as the Catholic Church hierarchy had been doing. Jägerstätter finally was getting the recognition of having been one the most courageous Austrian resisters against the Nazi regime during World War II that he deserved.

In the 1990s the Austrian public began to take note of the record of Austrian perpetrators during World War II (700,000 Austrian had been Nazi Party members and 1,200.000 million had served in the Wehrmacht). The Austrian government finally abandoned the "victims doctrine" and now admitted that Austrians bore "co-responsibility" for Hitlerite war crimes.[8] As a consequence, the study of the Austrian resistance, which for so long had dominated World War II studies in Austria, fell by the wayside and its record became understudied or ignored.[9] Austrian "mastering of its past" and Jägerstätter's beatification by

---

8 Cornelius Lehnguth, Waldheim und die Folgen: Der parteipolitische Umgang mit dem Nationalsozialismus in Österreich (Frankfurt a.M.-New York: Campus, 2013).

9 Neugebauer, Austrian Resistance, 20.

the Vatican helped resistance studies to rebound. Wolfgang Neugebauer's judicious study of the Austrian resistance finally gave Jägerstätter his due and put him on the cover of the English translation of the book as one of the best known Austrians who refused to budge to Nazi oppression. The 2005 symposium on the Austrian resistance staged in the Austrian Parliament was a further government-sponsored event to resurrect the record of the Austrian resistance as a central piece in Austria's World War II memory; Jägerstätter was given his due.[10]

Felix Mitterer's thoughtful play published here in an English translation for the first time, will add to Franz Jägerstätter's standing in the annals of conscientious objectors in the Austrian resistance. The play humanizes the man by stressing his inner conflicts in arriving at his bold decision not to join the Wehrmacht. It demonstrates how little time it took after the takeover of Austria ("Anschluss") in 1938 for the oppressive Nazi regime to nest itself into the deepest provinces of the renamed "Ostmark." Mitterer does not hesitate to show the cravenness of the Catholic church hierarchy. Mitterer also intimates that the postwar community of Sankt Radegund remained hostile to Jägerstätter's widow Franziska, blaming her for Franz's stubborn resistance to the Nazi regime and his "senseless" death. Finally Mitterer's play raises troubling issues about the morality of wars today and the need for conscientious objection for

10   Stefan Karner/Karl Duffek, eds., Widerstand in Östereich 1938-1945: Die Beiträge der Parlaments-Enquete 2005 (Graz-Vienna, 2007), 45f.

religiously faithful people. As long as governments draft ordinary citizens to serve in the wars they unleash, these questions will remain with us.

UNO Publishing is pleased to bring Mitterer's play to a wider readership in the English-speaking world. We would like to thank Zeno Stanek and Walter Kootz at Kaiser Verlag in Vienna for granting us permission to translate the play. We would also like to thank Erna Putz and the Archives of the Archdiocese of Linz for permission to use the photos of Franz Jägerstätter and his family from its holdings. Gregor Thuswaldner, Professor of German and Linguistics at Gordon College in Wenham, MA, originally brought the idea of publishing an English version to Günter Bischof, who suggested that his series "Studies in Central European History, Culture & Literature" with UNO Publishing might be a good fit for an English translation. Thuswaldner prepared a first draft of the translation and Robert Dassanowsky, Professor of German and Film Studies at the University of Colorado, Colorado Springs, went over it and helped improve it. Jeff Miller, Professor of Theater at Gordon College, offered helpful suggestions towards the end of the translation process. The Austrian Cultural Forum in New York supported the translation project with a grant. The Austrian-American Institute of the Botstiber Foundation helped the publication process along with a grant to UNO Publishing. We are grateful to Ambassador Christine Moser and her Deputy Director Christian-Joseph Ebner at the

Austrian Cultural Forum New York, as well as Terry Kline and the board members of Botstiber's Austrian-American Institute for their support. At UNO Publishing, Abram Himelstein and G.K. Darby have adopted this project with enthusiasm and Alex Dimeff has designed the cover and the book. At Center Austria, Gertraud Griessner carried on with the daily work and held Günter Bischof's back free to shepherd this project through to publication.

NEW ORLEANS, MAY 2015

INTRODUCTION

Gregor Thuswaldner

The heroic life and tragic death of Franz Jägerstätter (1907-1943), an Austrian farmer, remained obscured until decades after his demise. A devout Catholic, Jägerstätter was executed by the Nazis in 1943 as he, unlike the vast majority of the 1.3 million Austrians that were drafted between 1938 and 1945, refused to fight in Hitler's *Wehrmacht* because of his faith. Jägerstätter, however, did not take part in any religiously motivated resistance movements;[1] on the contrary, both his priest and bishop urged him to fight on Germany's side in World War II.[2]

After the war, many Austrians attempted to avoid the fact that Austria was part of Hitler's Third Reich. In 1938, according to Nazi officials 99.73% of all Austrians had voted to join Germany and to subjugate themselves under German rule.[3] When Germany annexed Austria and Hitler came to Vienna in March 1938, he was greeted by between 60,000 and 80,000 Austrians when he declared that

---

1 Erika Weinzierl provides a good overview of Austrian resistance. See Erika Weinzierl, "Resistance, Persecution, Forced Labor," in *Austria in the Twentieth Century*, ed. Rolf Steininger, Günter Bischof and Michael Gehler (New Brunswick: Transaction, 2002), 137-160.

2 On the varying Catholic responses in Austria regarding Hitler, see Evan Burr Bukey, *Hitler's Austria: Popular Sentiment in the Nazi Era* (Chapel Hill. University of North Carolina Press, 2000), 93-111.

3 The high number was clearly manipulated. See Bukey, 38.

his homeland of Austria was now part of the Reich.[4] Since Austria did not officially exist between 1938 and 1945, Austrian politicians blamed Germany for the war and its devastating consequences. They could also cite Austria's State Treaty of 1955, which referred to the so-called Moscow Declaration of 1943, a document that attempted to strengthen the resistance movements in Austria during the Third Reich. Drafted by the foreign secretaries of the Soviet Union, the United States, and Great Britain, the declaration stated that Austria was "the first free country to fall victim to Hitlerite aggression." Unlike the Moscow Declaration, however, the State Treaty did not insist on Austria's responsibility "which she cannot evade, for participation in the war on the side of Hitlerite Germany."[5]

As a consequence, for decades Austrian politicians refused to take responsibility for Austria's involvement in the Third Reich. Heidemarie Uhl has pointed out that despite the myth of Austria as the first victim of Hitler's Third Reich, Austrian soldiers who died during World War II were officially viewed as "dutiful and courageous heroes." In the 1950's and 1960's war memorials were set up throughout Austria supporting the positive portrayal of the soldiers of World War II. The monuments "expressed the idea that 'the homeland' was again standing by its sons

---

4   Ibid, 29.

5   Charles I. Bevans, ed., *Treaties and Other International Agreements of the United States of America: 1776-1949*, Vol. III. 1931-1945 (Washington, DC: Department of State, 1969), 827.

who fell in fierce battle by renewing and redesigning war memorials."[6]

Not surprisingly, most literary works written before the 1980's in Austria do not refer to the Holocaust or to war crimes committed by the Wehrmacht or any other Nazi forces. In his autobiographically inspired account *An Indication of the Cause* (1975), the famous Austrian author Thomas Bernhard echoes the prevailing belief that all Austrians were victims of the war: "At this time I was confronted by the sight of hundreds of men who had been wounded in the war, soldiers mutilated in battle; I became aware of the utter stupidity and obscenity of war and of the wretched plight of its victims."[7] The view that all Austrians were mere victims of the Second World War and of Hitlerite aggression dominated the public discourse in Austria until the mid 1980's. In 1949 Rosa Jochmann, a socialist politician, stated in a radio broadcast:

> We were all victims of fascism. Victim was the soldier, who experienced the war at the front in its most terrible form. Victim was the population who was waiting in the hinterland full of horror for the call of the cuckoo in order to flee to their shelters and

---

6   Heidemarie Uhl, "Transformation of Austrian Memory: Politics of History and Monument Culture in the Second Republic," *Austrian History Yearbook*, XXXII (2001), 160.

7   Thomas Bernhard, *Gathering Evidence*, trans. David McLintock (New York: Vintage, 1986), 107.

who, with longing, wished for the day which would take this fright from them. Victims were those who had to leave their native country to carry the mostly sad lot of the emigrant. Finally, we were victims, who in prisons, penitentiaries and concentration camps were defenseless prey of the SS.[8]

Austrians in general were seen as victims and fallen soldiers as heroes, resistance fighters and deserters were regarded as traitors. Consequently, Franz Jägerstätter, who was executed by the Nazis in 1943 for his refusal to fight for Hitler, was not seen in a positive light by Austrian authorities after 1945. Franz's widow, Franziska, did not receive the financial support other widows and orphans obtained from the state. Moreover, the townspeople of Sankt Radegund, Jägerstätter's hometown, openly criticized him for his alleged stubbornness as the reason for his demise.

According to the historian Helmut Konrad, between 4,000 and 5,000 Austrian resistance fighters were killed during the Nazi years while about 100,000 opponents of the Third Reich were incarcerated.[9] Unlike other

8   Brigitte Bailer, "They Were All Victims: The Selective Treatment of the Consequences of National Socialism, in Austrian Historical Memory and National Identity," Austrian Contemporary Studies Vol. 5, ed. Günter Bischof and Anton Pelinka (New Brunswick: Transaction, 1997), 106.

9   Helmut Konrad, "Righteous and Courageous in the Face of Nazism: Austrian Resistance against the Nazis: Myths and Realities," accessed April 4, 2015, http://www.doew.at/cms/download/dhm7u/konrad.pdf.

Austrians who fought the Nazi regime, Jägerstätter was not part of a larger movement. And unlike many resistance fighters, Jägerstätter was not highly educated. Despite the fact that he had only received an eight-year education in a one-classroom school in his hometown of Sankt Radegund, Franz read the newspaper on a regular basis and especially, beginning in the 1930's, the Bible. His letters and writings from prison reveal his deep faith, his striving for holiness, his remarkable theological reflections based primarily on the New Testament, and his insightful pacifistic political views. But this does not mean that Franz had always lived a saintly life in accordance with the moral teachings of the Catholic Church. As a teenager he did not stand out as morally superior from his peers; but rather he was known for his occasional brawls. His short-lived relationship with Theresia Bauer, a servant maid, resulted in the birth of a daughter, Hildegard in 1933. According to his first biographer, Gordon Zahn, this incident "might well have been the event which shocked the relatively wild youth into a personal conviction of sin and forced him into a totally new confrontation with Christianity as it affects one's moral obligations."[10] From that point on, Franz was committed to his faith and it resulted in his marriage to Franziska Schwaninger, an equally devout Christian in 1936. As a couple, they were as devoted to their Catholic faith as they were to each other. Unlike typical newlyweds

10   Gordon Zahn, *In Solidary Witness: The Life and Death of Franz Jägerstätter* (Springfield, IL: Templegate, 1984), 39.

in Sankt Radegund, Franz and Franziska spent their honeymoon on a pilgrimage to Rome, an experience they vowed to repeat every ten years. Moreover, Franz's commitment to his faith was coupled with his rejection of National Socialism.

In January 1938, Franz had a nightmare which he interpreted as profoundly prophetic. He dreamt about a seemingly beautiful train going around a mountain when, all of a sudden, adults as well as children began running towards the train in an eager attempt to get on it. Franz heard a voice saying: "This train is going to hell." Someone took Franz by his hand and told him: "Now we are going to purgatory." In his account, Franz did not elaborate much on the terrible suffering he saw and experienced in the dream.[11] This powerful image, which he interpreted as the fate of the National Socialist movement, remained with him. In his notebook of 1942, Franz wrote: "I want to cry out to all who are on this train: 'Jump off, before this train arrives at your final destination, even if it costs your life!' That is why I believe that through this dream or epiphany, which God has shown me and put in my heart, I could decide between National Socialism and Catholicism!"[12]

Jägerstätter's remarkable life story and his courage to resist the Nazi regime would have remained unknown to the larger public, had the American sociologist Gordon

---

11 Erna Putz, *Gefängnisbriefe und Aufzeichnungen: Franz Jägerstätter verweigert 1943 den Wehrdienst* (Linz: Veritas, 1987), 124.

12 Ibid, 127.

Zahn not stumbled upon his history while conducting research in Germany in 1956/57. In 1964, Zahn would publish *In Solitary Witness: The Life and Death of Franz Jägerstätter*, which attracted a significant readership and even influenced Vietnam War protesters in the United States. The Catholic Church in America ultimately referred to Jägerstätter's martyrdom when it issued numerous formal objections against the Vietnam War. As Zahn writes in the revised edition of his book two decades later,

> It is not too much to suggest that this humble peasant [i.e. Jägerstätter] changed the course of our history a generation later and an ocean away. On several occasions, speaking to college audiences, Daniel Ellsberg has revealed that this account of moral resistance unto death was one of the factors leading to his decision to release the Pentagon Papers. There is little doubt that this act and its effect upon public opinion hastened the end of this nation's involvement in that inglorious struggle.[13]

In other words, the life and death of the Austrian Franz Jägerstätter had a remarkable impact on American foreign policy, American public life, and even the teachings of the Catholic Church. During the Second Vatican Council, Archbishop Thomas Robert, discussed Jägerstätter's refusal to fight for Hitler even though he had been urged to do so by his priest and bishop. As a result, the Catholic Church

---

13   Zahn, iv.

officially recognized conscientious objectors for the first time. In *Gaudium et Spes*, the final document of the Second Vatican Council, the Church declared, "We cannot fail to praise those who renounce violence in vindication of their rights and who resort to methods of defense which are otherwise available to weaker parties too, provided this can be done without injury to the rights and duties of others or to the community itself."[14]

Styria, a Catholic press, published the German translation of Zahn's book in Austria in 1967. In 1972, Austrian director Axel Corti created *Verweigerung: Der Fall Jägerstätter* (*The Refusal: The Jägerstätter Case*), a docudrama for the Austrian national television network ORF, which introduced Jägerstätter to an even larger audience. Hellmut Andics's script for the film was based on Jägerstätter's letters and writings and it also included interviews with citizens of Sankt Radegund, who refused to see him as a martyr. As Robert Dassanowsky and Oliver Speck have correctly pointed out, the film was "a rare attempt at exploring dissident life in Austria during the Third Reich."[15] A decade following the release of *The Refusal*, Maximilian Aichern was named Bishop of Linz and because of Aichern, the Diocese recognized Franz's martyrdom publically.

---

14 Jim Forest, introduction to *Franz Jägerstätter: Letters and Writings from Prison*, ed. Erna Putz, transl. Robert A. Krieg (Maryknoll: Orbis, 2009), xi.

15 Robert Dassanowsky and Oliver Speck, "New Austrian Film: The Non-exceptional Exception," in *New Austrian Film*, ed. Robert Dassanowsky and Oliver Speck (New York: Berghahn, 2011), 7.

Over time, Jägerstätter's initially ambivalent image in Austria—hero for some, traitor for others—became more positive, despite the fact that some war veterans remained highly critical. When Jägerstätter's eightieth birthday was celebrated in the cathedral in Linz in 1987, a war veteran wrote the following in a letter to the editor of his local paper: "Only in Austria is such a person rewarded for his cowardice, for the betrayal of his comrades. Let Jägerstätter rest in peace; he deserved his fate."[16] Despite the fact that many Austrian Catholics thought along those same lines, the conference of Austrian bishops in 1992 supported Aichern's petition to beatify Franz Jägerstätter.

To underscore Jägerstätter's life and death on a more national scale Austria issued a postage stamp commemorating him in 1993. The stamp features a portrayal of the farmer from Sankt Radegund, the dates of his birth and death as well as the phrase "Er folgte seinem Gewissen" (He followed his conscience). Ultimately, Pope Benedict XVI officially beatified Jägerstätter in 2007. In his speech, Benedict praised Jägerstätter's courage and stressed the fact that Jägerstätter was neither a trained theologian nor an intellectual:

There are those who say human beings, particularly those without much formal education, cannot distinguish between right and wrong: Let them come to St.

---

16 Donald J. Moore, "Franz Jägerstätter: Conscience vs. Duty," *America*, February 19, 1994.

Radegund! There are those who say that individual human beings haven't the competence to determine whether a war is just or unjust, that this is the prerogative of "legitimate authority:" Let them come to St. Radegund! There are those who say that individual human beings ought not to refuse to participate in an unjust war—or other morally grievous wrongdoing—at the cost of their lives: Let them come to St. Radegund![17]

Since 2007, Franz Jägerstätter's reputation as a martyr has grown even stronger and the number of books, pamphlets, and educational materials dedicated to Jägerstätter's resistance has continued to multiply. His martrydom has also inspired theatrical adaptations of his life. Alexander Kratzer's one-woman show *Franziska Jägerstätter erzählt* (Franziska Jägerstätter recounts) received glowing reviews when it debuted in Linz in 2010. Actress Eike Baum was awarded Upper Austria's prestigious theater award for her powerful portrayal of Franziska.[18]

In 2011, actor Gregor Bloéb asked his friend, Felix Mitterer (*1948), one of Austria's most celebrated contemporary playwrights, to compose a drama for him about Franz Jägerstätter. At the time, Bloéb was artistic director of the

---

17   James Thunder "Pope Benedict's Surprise," *New Oxford Review*, March 2009, 31

18   Other lesser known literary adaptations include Martin Winkelbauer's play *Das Vermächtnis* (1989) and Kurt Benesch's novel *Die Suche nach Jägerstätter. Ein biographischer Roman* (1993).

Theatersommer Haag, a theater festival in Lower Austria. In his preface to Jägerstätter, Mitterer writes about his reluctance to fulfill his friend's wish as he was intimidated by Corti's impressive film and Kurt Weinzierl's performance of Jägerstätter. He was also doubtful that Bloéb, who was primarily known for his outgoing personality, would be able to convincingly portray Jägerstätter. However, three factors eventually helped change Mitterer's mind. While reading up on Jägerstätter's life and death, Mitterer was surprised to discover that Franz had not been a depressive or pietistic outsider but was very popular among the citizens of Sankt Radegund—at least until his conversion experience. Mitterer was also impressed by the love story between Franz and Franziska. And finally, Mitterer was moved by the fact that Franz's sacrifice had inspired conscientious objectors worldwide, particularly in the U.S. during the Vietnam War.[19]

Since the publication of his first play, *Kein Platz für Idioten* (*No Place for Idiots*) in 1974, Mitterer has been regarded as one of the leading Austrian playwrights. His many literary awards include the Ernst Toller Prize, the Adolf Grimme Prize, and most recently the Ödön von Horvath Prize. His dramatic works and film scripts are particularly well known for their critique of Austrian politics and society. Despite his popularity in Austria, Mitterer has not been adequately recognized beyond German-speaking Europe. One reason might be the folkloristic undertones

---

19 See Felix Mitterer "Mein Weg zu Franz Jägerstätter," in Felix Mitterer *Jägerstätter* (Innsbruck: Heymon, 2013), 5-9.

of his plays, which might be alienating to non-natives.[20] Another factor is the difficulty translators are faced with when it comes to Mitterer's use of language. In many of his plays, which are set in Tyrol, Mitterer's characters tend to speak non-standard varieties of Austrian-German. This is also the case in *Jägerstätter*, albeit to a lesser extent. It is unfortunate that Mitterer's work, which centers on universal themes of identity, gender relations and religion, is often misunderstood as too specifically regional because of its Alpine setting. This has contributed to the false impression that Mitterer's plays cannot be understood apart from its rural Austrian milieu.

Nevertheless, *Jägerstätter* stands out among his other plays for at least two reasons: On the one hand, unlike most of his other protagonists, *Jägerstätter* is based on the life history of a highly regarded individual who is now well known far beyond Austria. The play does not presuppose any particular regional or cultural knowledge. On the other hand, the play's theme—following one's conscience rather than doing one's duty—is recognized as a basic human right. In other words, it is safe to assume that the intensity of *Jägerstätter* and its thought-provoking message can and will be appreciated in very different cultural contexts.

---

20 As Karl E. Webb correctly writes "Mitterer's plays to a large extent, draw heavily upon his native Tyrol and its culture and traditions for their themes and structure." See Karl E. Webb, "An Introduction to Felix Mitterer and his Critics," in *Felix Mitterer: A Critical Introduction,* ed. Nicholas J. Meyerhofer (Riverside: Ariadne, 1995), 1.

The play was an instant success upon its premier on June 20, 2013 at Vienna's renowned Theater an der Josefstadt. Gregor Bloéb's portrayal of Franz Jägerstätter earned him a 2013 Nestroy Award, Austria's most respected theater prize, in the category of Best Male Actor. In their reviews, Austrian and German critics alike, praised the actors for their true-to-life and powerful performances as well as for Mitterer's unsentimental, yet sympathetic portrayal of Jägerstätter.

In the hands of a less capable playwright, *Jägerstätter* might have become a modern-day passion play filled with platitudes. But Mitterer, who incorporates passages from Jägerstätter's letters and writings from prison in his work, depicts Franz as a struggling and insecure human being—and not at all as anyone's idea of a saint. In fact, Mitterer's protagonist is a flawed character, who was frequently involved in bar fights and had fathered a child out of wedlock. In his introductory remarks in the German edition of his play, Mitterer points out that Franz was anything but a religious fanatic or a would-be intellectual. He was both spirited and adventurous, and a loving husband and father of four young girls. In other words, Franz was an unlikely candidate to challenge the political and religious authorities of the Nazi era. What makes Mitterer's play particularly compelling is its focus on Jägerstätter's discordant environment, namely on his friends and relatives, as well as on his priest and bishop who repeatedly urge him not to follow his conscience, but to take up arms in Hitler's army.

For Gordon Zahn, the Catholic Church failed Jäger-stätter, when it did not support his resistance:

> The German bishops' call for loyal service to folk and fatherland in World War II—as a Christian duty!—is a blasphemy that must never again be repeated by any clergyman, in any nation. So, too, with the pious cliché on which [Adolf] Eichmann based his plea. It must be replaced by the formal recognition that though obedience *can be* a virtue, *unquestioning or blind obedience*, even in an objectively good cause, is always a vice. The individual's obligation to make a responsible moral choice is never to be betrayed or denied.[21]

At the conclusion of the play, Mitterer reminds us that Jägerstätter should not be seen as an historical play without any connections to the present. According to the con-cluding stage directions, the audience listens to deafening explosions, shootings, and screams while the images pro-jected on the stage display contemporary acts of barbarism rather than historical images of war. The play's message is unmistakable: Franz Jägerstätter's principles and the trage-dy of his persecution is no less important today than it was during World War II.

---

21   Zahn, Gordon. *Conscience and Obedience, in Austria, 1938-1988: Anschluss and Fifty Years*, ed. William E. Wright (Riverside: Ariadne, 1995), 207.

Bibliography

Bailer, Brigitte. "They Were All Victims: The Selective Treatment of the Consequences of National Socialism," in *Austrian Historical Memory and National Identity*, Austrian Contemporary Studies Vol. 5, ed. Günter Bischof and Anton Pelinka (New Brunswick: Transaction, 1997), 103-115.

Bernhard, Thomas. *Gathering Evidence*, trans. David McLintock (New York, Vintage, 1986).

Bevans, Charles I. ed. *Treaties and Other International Agreements of the United States of America: 1776-1949*, Vol. III. 1931-1945 (Washington, DC: Department of State, 1969).

Bukey, Evan Burr. *Hitler's Austria: Popular Sentiment in the Nazi Era* (Chapel Hill. University of North Carolina Press, 2000).

Dassanowsky, Robert and Oliver Speck. *New Austrian Film* (New York: Berghahn), 2011.

Konrad, Helmut. "Righteous and Courageous in the Face of Nazism: Austrian Resistance against the Nazis: Myths and Realities," accessed April 4, 2015 http://www.doew.at/cms/download/dhm7u/konrad.pdf.

Moore, Donald J. "Franz Jägerstätter: Conscience vs. Duty," *America*, February 19, 1994, 12-14.

Putz, Erna. *Gefängnisbriefe und Aufzeichnungen: Franz Jägerstätter verweigert 1943 den Wehrdienst* (Linz: Veritas, 1987).

Putz, Erna. *Franz Jägerstätter: Letters and Writings from Prison*, transl. Robert A. Krieg (Maryknoll: Orbis, 2009).

Thunder, James. "Pope Benedict's Surprise," *New Oxford Review*, March 2009, 30-32.

Uhl, Heidemarie, "Transformation of Austrian Memory: Politics of History and Monument Culture in the Second Republic," *Austrian History Yearbook*, XXXII (2001), 149-167.

Webb, Karl E. "An Introduction to Felix Mitterer and his Critics," in *Felix Mitterer: A Critical Introduction*, ed. Nicholas J. Meyerhofer, (Riverside: Ariadne, 1995), 1-18.

Weinzierl, Erika. "Resistance, Persecution, Forced Labor," in *Austria in the Twentieth Century*, ed. Rolf Steininger, Günter Bischof and Michael Gehler (New Brunswick: Transaction, 2002), 137-160.

Zahn, Gordon. *In Solidary Witness: The Life and Death of Franz Jägerstätter* (Springfield, IL: Templegate, 1984).

Zahn, Gordon. *Conscience and Obedience, in Austria, 1938-1988: Anschluss and Fifty Years*, ed. William E. Wright (Riverside: Ariadne, 1995), 197-208.

JÄGERSTÄTTER

Translated from the German language play by Felix Mitterer
by Gregor Thuswaldner with Robert Dassanowsky

CAST:

FRANZ JÄGERSTÄTTER
FRANZISKA, *his wife*
ROSALIA, *his mother*

THERESIA, *mother of Franz's child*
HEAD TEACHER, *local group leader*
PRIEST FÜRTHAUER
MAYOR
RUDI, *son of a farmer*

BISHOP OF LINZ
OFFICER, *older Colonel in Enns*

DR. FELDMANN, *officer and Franz's lawyer in Berlin*

All actors except for Franz and Franziska are part of the Chorus. The Coryphaeus alternates.

Franz's and Franziska's daughters are portrayed by dolls: Rosl (9/1/37), Maridl (9/4/38), Loisi (5/5/40). Also Hilde, Theresia's daughter (5 years old).

No swastika flags, no Nazi paraphernalia, no Nazi uniforms.

Leherbauer Farm in Sankt Radegund.

Franziska, Rosalia (Franz's mother), the three children Rosl, Maridl, Loisi.

Behind them motionless the Chorus (villagers).

Franziska holds a sealed envelope in her hand; she and Rosalia stare at it, expecting the worst. After a while, Franziska opens the envelope, takes out the letter, unfolds it and looks at it. Rosalia makes an impatient gesture.

FRANZISKA: (*reads*) Berlin-Brandenburg, August 9, 1943. Dear Frau Jägerstätter, Regretfully, I must inform you that today at 4PM your husband's verdict was executed. He confessed his sins very devoutly and spoke with me. He sent his heartfelt greetings to you and the children. He remained controlled and devout until the last moment. May our sorrowful Mother of God comfort you in your great heartache and may She help you to valiantly endure your lot and, now that your husband is dead, master all the tasks before you. Sincerely, Albert Jochmann.

Silence. Franziska and Rosalia are frozen. Rosalie yells terribly and begins hitting Franziska who is not defending herself.

ROSALIA: You killed him! You killed him! You killed him!

The Chorus surrounds Franziska.

CHORUS: You killed him! Killed. Killed.

ROSALIA: The bigot! Killing my son! My one and only! Murderer!

CHORUS: Bigot. Murderer. Killing her son.

Franziska grabs her children; they cling to her.

CORYPHAEUS: The coward!

CHORUS: The coward. The coward dog. The worst coward imaginable.

ROSALIA: He wasn't a coward! My Franz was not a coward!

FRANZISKA: He let himself be killed for his faith. Is that cowardly?

CORYPHAEUS: But he thought he could talk himself out of it.

CHORUS: Yes, talk himself out of it. Squirm himself free of it.

CORYPHAEUS: He was good at talking.

CHORUS: He was good at rambling.

ROSALIA: Such an intelligent man, my Franz. She made him crazy.

CHORUS: She made him crazy.

CORYPHAEUS: Nutcase. Public enemy. Traitor.

CHORUS: Nutcase. Public enemy. Traitor.

CORYPHAEUS: Abandons his family. Abandons his children.

CHORUS: Abandons his family. Abandons his children. Abandons his homeland.

CORYPHAEUS: Thinks he's something special, believes he's a saint.

FRANZISKA: He is a saint! The only one who said no. One day you will see that he was right.

CORYPHAEUS: And our sons are wrong?

CHORUS: Our sons and brothers and fathers are wrong?

CORYPHAEUS: All those who risked their lives are wrong?

FRANZISKA: Yes, they are wrong! And Franz risked his life, not your fathers' and brothers' and sons'!

CORYPHAEUS: My son was killed in action!

CHORUS: My son was killed in action! My brother was killed in action! My father was killed in action!

FRANZISKA: I am sorry about that. I am terribly sorry about that.

Coryphaeus: Everyone has to do his duty, everyone.

Chorus: For the fatherland, for the great fatherland.

Coryphaeus: Führer command, we follow you.

Chorus: One People, One Reich, One Leader.

Coryphaeus: People rise up and let the storm break loose.

Franziska: Madness! Madness!

Coryphaeus: He brought shame over us.

Chorus: He brought shame and dishonor to our village.

Franziska: Thou shalt not kill. Thou shalt love thy neighbor! What kind of Christians are you?

Coryphaeus: We are Christians.

Chorus: We are Christians, but we're also men.

Coryphaeus: Righteous men.

Chorus: What kind of a man is your husband?

Rosalia: It's her fault! She made him weak! What a man he once was!

Coryphaeus: What a man!

Chorus: What a man! Chasing women, the strongest brawler in town, the best bowler in town, racing down the highways with his motorcycle.

ROSALIA: She made him weak, she made him small.

FRANZISKA: Great is Franz, much greater than all of you. As great as the firmament.

CORYPHAEUS: He's not that great anymore.

CHORUS: He's not so great anymore, in any case he's a head shorter now.

FRANZISKA: Stop it! I can't take it anymore! Franz! Franz!

2.

1933.

Leherbauer Farm.

Franz and his mother, Rosalia.

Behind them Theresia, standing, advanced in pregnancy.

FRANZ: She can work hard, mother! Everybody says so! And we need **one** who can work hard!

ROSALIA: Come on, Franz. Look, a farmer's daughter brings a dowry to your family. We could use such a girl. Necessary, absolutely necessary. I can't even afford my own health insurance. They will auction the farm.

FRANZ: And why don't we have money? Why? The farmer does stupid things. He has an enormous chicken farm, nobody buys our chickens, nobody buys our eggs. Everyone in the region has their own chickens. He could harvest the fields properly. I can't do it all by myself. And as soon as he gets a few coins, he spends them on booze.

ROSALIA: He is seriously ill, a desperate man. And don't say farmer, he is your father.

FRANZ: He's not my father.

ROSALIA: Yes, your adoptive father, don't start this again.

We should be thankful for him.

FRANZ: But I'm still an unpaid laborer who has to beg for every coin.

ROSALIA: You will inherit the farm. Then you will own the Leherbauer Farm. It's the only desire of my life. My boy will become a farmer.

FRANZ: Can I finally bring Theresia in here now?

Rosalia making a weary gesture. Franz approaching Theresia.

FRANZ: Resi! You coming?

They go inside. Rosalia looks at Theresia's pregnant stomach. She gestures that they should sit down. They sit down.

ROSALIA: Who are you?

THERESIA: I'm Theresia Auer from Bürmoos.

ROSALIA: Bürmoos. By the moor people. The poorest part of Salzburg.

THERESIA: (*nodding*) The absolute poorest part. My father cut peat. Not alive anymore. The moor ate him.

ROSALIA: Who are you working for?

THERESIA: For the Farmer Schirk. In the stable.

ROSALIA: A stable maid.

Theresia: Yes. You were one too, right?

Rosalia: (*ignoring her comment*) You're still working?

Theresia: Until yesterday. The farmer says I can't anymore. I shouldn't lose my child in his stable.

Rosalia: You're a hard-working girl, I hear. (*Long pause, to Theresia*) But we need one with money. Otherwise we can't go on.

Franz: I can't abandon Resi, mother!

Rosalia: Vroni Gwirl has her eye on you. Her father is the richest farmer in town.

Franz: Am I not able to choose my own wife?

Rosalia: No, you are not allowed to. You have a responsibility. Just like me. I married a sick man because of you. And now **you** are making a sacrifice! (*To Theresia*) No hard feelings.

Theresia gets up and walks out.

Franz: Resi! Wait for me! (*Wants to go after her.*)

Rosalia: Who knows if the child is really yours.

Franz: (*pauses*) It is mine! Don't talk her down, alright!

Rosalia: Who cares? She wouldn't be the first stable maid who claims a farmer is the father and now he has to marry her.

FRANZ: Stop it now, mother! She's not like that!

ROSALIA: If you take her, I will tell your stepfather he should bequeath the farm to some other relative.

FRANZ: Go sit on a tack, both of you! I'm going to Eisenerz. I can earn a lot of money there. And I can marry who I want.

ROSALIA: Franz, you are a farmer, you are not suited for blast furnaces. Must you really have her? Are you that infatuated with her? (*Franz does not answer.*) Now what? Come on. Be honest.

FRANZ: I don't go crazy if I don't see her. But I can't abandon her.

ROSALIA: I'll pay the child support for you, Franz. From my egg money.

FRANZ: (*struggles with himself*) No! No, mother, that's not right. To take advantage of a poor girl. (*He goes outside. Theresa stands there. She is sad and does not look at him.*)

FRANZ: Resi. Do you really like me? A lot?

THERESA: Yes, I like you, Franz.

FRANZ: So much that you want to stay with me for life?

THERESIA: Why are you talking like the priest in church? I like you, you're nice and I'd rather be a farmer's wife than a stable maid. (*Franz looks at her, then looks away.*) You farmers always think a stable maid is easy game. Is that the case with you, too?

FRANZ: No, not easy, no. But I was wild about you, I admit that.

THERESA: I was wild about you, too. And then you had me and now it's over? Good enough for the haystack but not good enough for the farm.

FRANZ: I don't think that way. (*Searches for words.*) I just think, I have to like a woman so completely, also her beliefs on the inside. So that my heart leaps when I see her. So that I only feel complete when we're together. (*Theresia begins to cry. He is speechless and empathetic; he wants to touch her, she pushes him away.*) I don't know you, Resi. I don't know you enough, so that I could know that.

THERESIA: How do you want to know me? How does that work? A stable maid doesn't even get Sundays off, you know that. In the morning in the stable, at night in the stable. In between time for Sunday mass, then lunch, then we meet for two hours in the haystack. For two hours, so nobody will find out about us, and then back to work. How do you want to get to know me? Is it my fault? That's a farm laborer's life!

FRANZ: Resi, let it be. I'll marry you.

THERESIA: God bless, I don't need your pity. (*Goes away, turns around.*) Now I'm giving birth to the child. My mother, who doesn't know anything—who runs to church every single day and thinks that a child out of wedlock is a deadly sin, she will hopefully give me a bed. Otherwise I'll give birth in the stable. Wouldn't be the first time that a child is born in a stable, would it? (*Walks off.*)

FRANZ (*calls after her*): I will always take care of the child, Resi, I promise. Not just with money. As her father—forgive me, please.

3.

At the Pub. Franz is in a bad mood alone at a table, beer in front of him, smoking a cigarette. Farmers (Chorus) are also drinking beer at other tables, among them Rudi, son of a rich farmer. All are wearing hats. Franz ignores the following provocation as long as possible.

Rudi: Hey, where is this stench coming from?

Chorus: What stench, Rudi?

Rudi: It smells like chicken shit, doesn't it?

Chorus: (*sniffing*) You're right, Rudi, you're right. Could be chicken shit.

Rudi: Did anyone not clean their shoes?

Chorus: (*looking at their soles*) We don't have any chicken shit on our shoes.

Rudi: (*sniffing, points over his shoulder at Franz*) It's coming from over there.

Chorus: Oh, from over there.

Rudi: It's coming from the chicken farmer.

Chorus: The Farmer Leher stinks like that?

Rudi: Come on, go and air yourself out, chicken farmer.

Franz turns slowly towards them.

CHORUS: Chicken farmer is getting upset.

RUDI: No hard feelings, chicken farmer. (*Franz gets up, throws a coin on the table and leaves.*) Wait a minute, chicken farmer. Wanted to ask you something.

CHORUS: Just a minute. He wants to ask you something. (*Franz turns around.*)

RUDI: A stable maid is walking through our village. With such (*makes a gesture*) a stomach. Was that you?

CHORUS: Oh, it was Franz?

RUDI: A farmer's daughter wouldn't let him near her.

CHORUS: Are you sure, Rudi? That a farmer's daughter wouldn't let him get near her.

RUDI: Everybody knows he's a servant's bastard.

CHORUS: Yes, we all know that. But now he's a farmer.

RUDI: Chicken farmer. As long as he's not breeding rabbits like the peasants. (*Franz can hardly control himself.*)

CHORUS: Franz, you're putting up with a lot today. (*Franz turns away again in order to leave.*)

RUDI: (*gets up*) Wait a minute, chicken farmer. I'm coming to the point now.

CHORUS: Just a moment, Franz, he's coming to his point now. (*Franz turns around.*)

RUDI: It's about my trees.

CHORUS: Oh, it's about your trees?

FRANZ: What about your trees?

RUDI: Are you giving them back to me?

CHORUS: Oh, he wants his trees back.

FRANZ: What trees?

RUDI: The ones you cut down in my woods.

CHORUS: Oh, he cut trees down in your woods.

RUDI: He did. And quite a lot of them.

FRANZ: I didn't cut down any trees in your woods. Those were our trees.

RUDI: You're poor devils, I know, but I need the trees myself.

CHORUS: Right! Poor devils!

FRANZ: (*walks up to Rudi, stops in front of him*) They are our trees.

CHORUS: (*to the farmer*) Are they his trees?

RUDI: They are my trees. And I need them because I'm building a new farm house. And it needs a roof structure. You understand that, don't you?

CHORUS: Franz will certainly understand.

FRANZ: Don't piss me off! I didn't go beyond the property border.

RUDI: I'm sorry but I will have to take you to court. I absolutely need those trees.

CHORUS: He absolutely needs them.

RUDI: I want to get married before winter, you know.

CHORUS: Right! He's gonna get married!

RUDI: I'll marry Vroni Gwirl. You know her, Franz.

CHORUS: Right! Dammit, everybody would want Vroni Gwirl.

RUDI: And it shouldn't snow in the bedroom, right?

CHORUS: (*sings a stanza*)

If it snows in the bedroom

That would be bad.

That would be sad.

For the bride and the groom.

RUDI: I can understand that as a servant's bastard and a chicken farmer you don't know much about property borders but— (*As quick as a flash Franz punches the farmer down with only one punch.*)

CHORUS: (*cries out*) Ohhhhhhh! (*Rudi lies motionlessly on the floor. Franz stares at him, frightened.*) Bravo, Franz, you're the man. He was asking for it. (*Franz is leaving.*) Franz, stay, let's clink glasses. Franz!

4.

Church.

FRANZ: Holy Mother of God, let him survive. Holy Mother of God, let him survive. Holy Mother of God, let him survive. I get so furious, I know, I get so furious. When I feel it in my veins, I don't know myself anymore. But I have my honor. Do I have to be provoked by this son of a bitch? No, it's not about Vroni Gwirl, I couldn't care less about her. It's about the trees. I didn't cut them down but my stepfather did. The drunk probably got the wrong ones. (*Pulls out the rosary.*) This is my grandmother's rosary. I'll pray seven rosaries, if he survives. It's not enough for you? If anyone strikes you on the cheek, turn the other also. I can't do that. Fourteen rosaries and I won't touch any girls for half a year. Is that enough? I'll go to Eisenerz to the blast furnace. An uncle of mine was there. I'll have to earn money. And hopefully, the whole thing will be alright. I need to tell you about my uncle. He's not alive anymore because he hanged himself in Eisenerz. He was the opposite of me. Hit his wife when he was drunk and when he was sober again he said that a man who hits his woman doesn't have right to live. And so he hanged himself. I'm not going to hang myself. Sorry. But I promise you that I will restrain myself in the future. I'd better go now. Thank you for listening. (*Bends his knee and crosses himself, leaves.*)

5.

Blast furnace at Eisenerz. Fiery, hellish furnace, glowing sparks flying, hellish noise. The Chorus as workers. Franz is among them. Siren—change of shift.

The workers come to the front; others come and resume working at their work place. Silence.

Socialists gather on the left, the Nazis on the right. Franz in the middle. He has a piece of paper in his hand, stiffly reading his poem.

FRANZ: Don't be too proud, you rich man, as you too will also die.

Applause from both sides.

CHORUS: Bravo! You too will also die.

Franz: (*continues*) Give up the evil class struggle.

The chorus on the left is irritated; the one on the right applauds.

CHORUS ON THE RIGHT: Give up the evil class struggle.

FRANZ: (*continues*) Because God's Son did not find his riches on earth. (*Both Choruses refuse to listen.*)
Oh how are our days filled with pain,
On our short street car ride
Which we all ride unequally.

CHORUS ON THE LEFT: Which we all ride unequally.

FRANZ: Until the train derails.
Now I ask you, oh proud man,
If personal wealth is enough
As long as God gives you health
And you have no care.

The Chorus on the right sighing exasperatedly.

FRANZ: But all the nice gifts
Don't bring you the luck you had hoped for.
If you lack love in your heart
Because it too is a masterpiece.

Both Choruses sighing exasperatedly.

Franz: And peace and love don't last for a long time,
If you don't believe in your God
And in any eternity. (*Franz stands in an awkward pose, looks at the workers.*)

NAZI WORKERS: Spare us with your poems! We don't want anything to do with your god! The Führer is our God!

SOCIALIST WORKERS: Spare us with your poems! We don't want anything to do with your eternity! Death to capitalists!

CHORUS ON THE RIGHT: (*"The Führer" by Herbert Böhme.*)
A drum can be heard in Germany
And the one who plays it is the leader

And those who follow him, follow silently.
They are chosen by him.
They swear the oath of allegiance,
Loyalty and justice.
With a stern face
He blazes the trail of their fate.
Determined he marches towards the sun
With fierce power.
His drum, Germany, is you!
People, become passionate!

CHORUS ON THE LEFT: (*"The March of the Calves" by Bertolt Brecht, written as a reaction to the previous poem.*)
Behind the drum
The calves trot
The skin for the drum
They offer themselves.
The butcher calls. The eyes are tightly shut.
The calf marches on with a calm steady step.
The calves, whose blood has already been shed in the slaughterhouse,
Follow in spirit along in its ranks.

Both Choruses attack each other with heavy tools; they run over Franz, a fierce fight breaks out. The siren sounds. Blackout.

6.

Pub " Zur Reib" in Ach. Franziska cleaning the tables in the restaurant. No customers. Franz approaches.

FRANZ: Franziska!

FRANZISKA: (*shakes his hand*) Hello, Franz. Don't you have anything to do at home?

FRANZ: Why?

FRANZISKA: Because this is your third time here **this** week.

FRANZ: It doesn't take longer than 15 minutes with my motorbike.

FRANZISKA: But around here no farmer goes to the pub during the week.

FRANZ: I'm here because of you not because of the beer. Want to ask you something.

FRANZISKA: And that can't wait until Sunday?

FRANZ: On Sunday the other fellows are here, too.

FRANZISKA: And then you would have to fight with them, right? Because you're chasing after girls in another village.

FRANZ: I'm not getting into fights anymore. And I'm only after one girl.

FRANZISKA: Since when?

FRANZ: Since I saw you. And I can't stand it if they stare at you, the other men. Do you **have** to be a waitress?

FRANZISKA: I'm not a waitress.

FRANZ: What then?

FRANZISKA: I pick up the bowling pins in my free time so I can earn some extra coins. That's it. And sometimes I help by pouring drinks when the place is packed. Otherwise I'm in the kitchen or in the stable. And a waitress is not an easy girl. I want to make that clear, Franz Jägerstätter. And besides: you men can go wild, but we girls are supposed to be chaste.

FRANZ: I didn't mean—

FRANZISKA: (*interrupts him*) You have a child out of wedlock, don't you?

FRANZ: C'mon, you already know that.

FRANZISKA: Of course, I know. Because I don't dance with a man twice if I don't know him. Why don't you marry your child's mother? Why did you abandon her?

FRANZ: I'm leaving.

FRANZISKA: No, we need to talk about it now. I asked you something.

FRANZ: It didn't feel right, we both felt that. (*She looks at him questioningly.*) And my mother didn't want me to marry a stable maid.

FRANZISKA: Oh, is that so? And the poor child has to pay for it?

FRANZ: I visit her almost every Sunday, my daughter Hilde. And I bring her sweets and apples and sausages for the grandmother. Then I take her for a ride on my motorbike. She likes that a lot.

FRANZISKA: Is she a nice girl, your Hilde?

FRANZ: Yes, she's quite active, a wild one. (*Smiles.*) Just like me. (*They look at each other.*) You're scolding me for racing on my motorbike to Maria Ach every third day, even though I'm the only one who can do the hard work at home on the farm. Don't you know the reason for it?

FRANZISKA: Then ask me what you want to ask me so that you can go back to work again.

FRANZ: Do you want to marry me? That's want I wanted to ask you. My mother would be in favor of it, too.

FRANZISKA: Because I'm a farmer's daughter and I have a dowry?

FRANZ: That's how she is. All that matters to me is that you are mine.

FRANZISKA: Why?

FRANZ: You read. (*Franziska laughs out loud.*) I saw you, often. With a book in your hand, back in the orchard. Every free minute you read. I do that too. One has to be informed about the world. Why do you read?

FRANZISKA: I suppose I take after my father. He used to read the entire newspaper and serialized novels to us on Sunday afternoons. And that's the only reason why I'm yours?

FRANZ: No, I also like you a lot as a girl.

FRANZISKA: Then I'm glad.

FRANZ: Me too. And you have such a beautiful smile.

FRANZISKA: You're also my dearest. But we've only known each other for a few months. Tell me something about you.

FRANZ: What do you want me to tell you?

FRANZISKA: You were born out of wedlock, right? Your mother was a stable maid, too. Like your child's mother. Right?

FRANZ: Yes, that's right. She was a stable maid and poor as a church mouse. And my father was a farm laborer and just as poor. That's why they couldn't get married. And my mother couldn't keep me. No farmer allows that, you know that. A maid with a child, that just can't be. That's why I spent ten years with my grandmother. Then the Farmer Leher married my mother and adopted me.

FRANZISKA: That was decent of the Farmer Leher.

FRANZ: Yes, it was a decent thing for him to do. He died half a year ago. Of tuberculosis.

FRANZISKA: May God comfort him.

FRANZ: So how is it to be? Are you taking me?

FRANZISKA: People say you lose your temper too often. Knocked someone down in the pub. You were jailed for it.

FRANZ: For three days. And I paid for damages. Only dislocated his chin. You know, fists from the Innviertel. I swore I would never do something like that again.

FRANZISKA: Do you go to church?

FRANZ: Of course, I go to church.

FRANZISKA: Because you like it or because it's customary?

FRANZ: When I was a child I liked to go with my grandmother. The incense and the lights, nobody's fighting, all pray together…Then when I was a young man I went because it was customary and because you can look at the girls for a long time…

FRANZISKA: (*smiles*) That's what I thought.

Franz: But now, I like going again. I was in Eisenerz, at the blast furnace. I got so confused because of all the politicizing. And then I got homesick. And I longed for our church. I mean our church in Radegund. Because it's so homey. I wanted to go back again. And I began reading the gospel. You can find everything about justice in it. And about neighborly love. I like that more than the political slogans.

Franziska: And you're sure about me?

Franz: Of course, that's why I'm telling you.

Franziska: Your adoptive father died, your mother is sick, you will have to take over the farm. You just need a farmer's wife.

Franz: But I wouldn't take just anybody because of that. I'm always so happy when I see you. I've never been as happy with any other girl.

Franziska: I will marry you then.

Franz: (*takes her hand*) God bless you, Franziska.

Franziska: God bless you too, Franzl. We will always like each other, right?

Franz: Always. (*Shouts for joy, lifts her up and kisses her.*)

The Chorus approaches.

CHORUS: Getting secretly married at six in the morning. And no wedding feast and no music band is playing, and they're not paying for our drinks. Such a poor wedding is unheard of around here.

CORYPHAEUS: And then they go on their honeymoon.

CHORUS: And then they go on their honeymoon. That's unheard of around here.

CORYPHAEUS: And where are they going?

CHORUS: And where are they going? To Altötting or Mariazell? No, they're off to Rome, to the Pope.

CORYPHAEUS: To Rome, to the Pope.

CHORUS: They think they're better than us, but as for paying for our drinks, no.

7.

Franz and Franziska holding Rosl (7 months) in her arm. Rosalia keeps a distance to them.

Franziska: (*with a newspaper*) You heard it yourself, it was read from the pulpit, what Cardinal Innitzer says and it's in the paper too. (*Reads.*) "For us bishops, it is a national duty to avow ourselves as Germans to the German Reich and we expect the same from all believing Christians."

Franz: He'll be surprised, our Herr Cardinal.

Rosalia: You're smarter than our Cardinal?

Franz: No, I'm not. But a cardinal is a politician. There's no other way, I guess. He probably made a deal with the Nazis. Whether they stick with it is a different thing altogether. You could see that in Germany.

Franziska: You have to go there, Franz.

Franz: No, I'm not going. Why do we need a referendum now that they've already invaded us, now that all the tanks are already here? That's a swindle, Fani.

Franziska: You can get in trouble, Franz.

Rosalia: You're so pigheaded.

Franz: I got that from you, Mother.

FRANZISKA: Just cast a blank ballot. Do it for me. And for Rosl.

FRANZ: Rosl, what do you say? Should I go? You see, she says no.

FRANZISKA: If you don't go, I won't like you anymore. (*He looks at her befuddled; she is startled by her own words.*)

ROSALIA: You don't say that, Fani. A good wife doesn't do that.

FRANZ: (*to Franziska*) What did you say?

ROSALIA: We farmers are most important to the Führer. We are the nutrition professionals, he says. Because of us we have bread. He promised us: no farmer will lose their farm. With Germany we are strong. (*Franz stares at her in horror.*)

ROSALIA: You're going and you're voting "yes." Otherwise I'm not your mother anymore.

FRANZISKA: (*appeasing*) Franz...I'm begging you. What is small Austria supposed to do? Fight against Germany?

FRANZ: I'm telling you, we will go under with Germany.— read his book, Franziska. Then you'll know everything. Read it. Then you'll know what the world is in for. What he will do to the world and to its people.

FRANZISKA: I don't want to read it.

ROSALIA: I've read it, Franz.

FRANZ: You? Since when do you read books?

ROSALIA: I've read it. And he's right in many ways.

FRANZ: I had a dream last night. About a train. An infinitely long train. Full of people. It departs slowly. And countless people are running for it and jumping on it. And they are yelling enthusiastically. A couple of people are waving to me to jump on as well. You were among them, mother. A nameless terror is befalling me, I'm paralyzed. No, I don't want to get on this train. Then all of a sudden a voice is telling me: "This train is going to hell." And I saw suffering, a suffering that the world had never seen before. An unfathomable horror. I didn't want to see it. I wished I was dead. Then I heard a boom, saw a glaring light, and everything was gone.

8.

Referendum, April 10, 1938

There are no booths for a secret ballot. The Chorus passes the ballot box to drop off their "yes" votes. The head teacher and two other members of the chorus are officials.

Franz, Franziska, and Rosalia approaching, take the ballots; Franziska looking at Franz, Franz not looking at her purposely, marks "no" and drops off the ballot. Franziska hesitates, not marking anything, and drops her blank ballot into the ballot box. Rosalia votes with yes, shows her ballot to one of the officials and drops the ballot in the ballot box. Franz wants to leave. The head teacher approaches him.

HEAD TEACHER: Jägerstätter.

FRANZ: Head Teacher or do I have to call you Local Group Leader?

HEAD TEACHER: Head Teacher is enough.

FRANZ: Yes, maybe it's better that way. As a teacher you have students, but you're a Local Group Leader without a local group.

Head Teacher: That will change. What I wanted to say: we need a new mayor badly.

FRANZ: Why? The old one is not good enough anymore?

HEAD TEACHER: Ultra conservative. Impossible. But I can't find anyone, nobody wants to take on responsibility. The authorities are threatening us with staffing the position with a Commissioner of their choosing. Should we allow that? You are a well-read and educated man. And you haven't had a political position. You won't attract attention. Don't you want to act as mayor?

Franz looks at him dumbfounded and then laughs. The head teacher is confused.

CORYPHAEUS: And here is the result of the vote. Sankt Radegund votes for the incorporation of Austria into the German Reich, one hundred percent.

CHORUS: One hundred percent.

HEAD TEACHER: I congratulate you all. We now belong to the unified and proud German national body.

CHORUS: Yes, German national body.

Franz walks up to the ballot box, searching it, not finding his ballot with his "No" vote. Franziska and Rosalia are worried.

ROSALIA: Franz, stop it, we're going home now.

Franz looks at the Coryphaeus, approaches him, searches his pockets, and finds the ballot with the "No" crossed and looks at it.

FRANZ: The German national body is not quite complete.

(*Holds up the ballot.*) No!

HEAD TEACHER: Now you are alone, Jägerstätter. It's not good to be alone.

FRANZ: (*to the Chorus*) Why are you doing that? I don't understand you. In Sankt Radegund there wasn't a single illegal Nazi. And now they can't find a mayor. We all know each other. And we are all the same: farmers and craftsmen. We are friends, good neighbors, who always help each other, almost all of us are somehow related. And all of us go to church on Sundays. And now you're saying yes to a man who is preparing for war.

CORYPHAEUS: (*amicably*) Franz, it is how it is. These are the times.

CHORUS: (*whispers*) It is how it is. These are the times.

CORYPHAEUS: How can a small village change that?

CHORUS: How can a small village change that?

CORYPHAEUS: Our "no" would not be heard.

CHORUS: Not be heard.

CORYPHAEUS: If we go unnoticed, nothing will happen to us.

CHORUS: Nothing will happen to us.

Franz: Something will happen.

Coryphaeus: The most important thing is that we look after each other.

Chorus: Look after each other, look after each other.

Head Teacher: I will have to report that, Jägerstätter. With your "no" vote, you are spitting at the Führer's feet.

Coryphaeus: Forget that, Head Teacher. We don't tell on anyone around here.

Chorus: Forget that. Forget that.

Head Teacher: As you like it. He will betray himself anyway. So then, one hundred percent. I will pass it on.

Chorus: One hundred percent.

9.

Franz, Franziska (with Rosl in her arm) and Theresia (with Hilde in her arm).

FRANZ: My, have you grown, Hilde! Look, I brought you some sweets. (*Puts them in Theresa's pocket.*) Hilde, this is Rosl, your sister. You'll like each other.

THERESA: Have you come because of the money?

FRANZ: What do you mean, what money?

THERESA: Your mother hasn't been paying the alimony. For months.

FRANZ: I am very embarrassed. I'm sorry.

FRANZISKA: Why does your mother pay alimony? What does **she** have to do with it?

FRANZ: She wanted it that way. How much do I owe you, Resi?

THERESA: 25 Schillings. I don't know how much that is in German Reichsmark.

FRANZ: I don't have that much on me.

THERESA: Don't forget it. So tell me, why have you come? And why are you bringing her? (*Points at Franziska.*)

Franz: We want to make you an offer.

Theresia: You two—an offer?

Franz: We want to adopt Hilde.

Theresia: You want to take my child from me?

Franz: No, we're not taking her away from you, Resi. She will be fine with us. She's going to be with a family. Not with an old woman in seclusion. An old reclusive woman. You can visit her, of course, as often as you want. Our place is closer to you than your mother's place.

Theresa: Go away. This is my child! My child! I don't need you. The Führer takes care of me. And for him a child is a child. And for him there is no such thing as a child of sin, like for you Catholics. Heil Hitler! (*Franziska departs sadly.*)

Franz: You will find a good man.

Theresia: I don't want to find a good man. I wanted you! (*Theresia departs. Franz looks at her sadly as she leaves, and then follows Franziska.*)

10.

Franz (backpack on his back, a hat on his head) taking Rosl for a walk in a stroller. When the members of the Chorus approach him, he tips his hat automatically.

FRANZ: What are you saying, Rosl? I should tell you a story? You want me to tell you stories all the time, but I can't always think of one. What do you want to hear?—I know something. Once upon a time, a couple of years ago, your father was all alone and lonely. He lived with his mother at the farm all alone and he only worked and read. He studied, Rosl, he studied books. About the world, about what's going on out there and about the saints, about the proclaimers of truth…

TWO MEMBERS OF THE CHORUS: (*pass by him*) Now he's walking around with a stroller. Has a farmer ever gone for a walk with a stroller around here? Now he's gone completely mad.

FRANZ: The neighbors laughed at him when they saw him read a book again in the field, or on the way home when he held a book in one hand the rope in the other hand…You know our grays, our pulling cows, we call them grays, they know the way themselves. A couple of neighbors thought your father was going mad and was neglecting his work on the farm because of all the reading, but none of that was true, not at all. But he almost became a hermit, your father, he hardly ever went to the pub, like in the past, all of a sudden it was just too loud for him...

Two Members of the Chorus: (*from the other side*) Now look at that! He's pushing a stroller. That's because he reads. Now he's gone completely mad.

Franz: Your father was missing a human being, another human being. And the following happened. In Hochburg, a village ten kilometers from here, a flower grew out of the soil, a very beautiful flower. First, only a bud and then it grew. It turned out tall and slim and on a beautiful morning in the spring it blossomed. The flower was yellow like the sun and had sky blue threads inside. It smelled so wonderful. Are you listening to me, Rosl? And your father smelled this sweet scent. It made him quite dizzy. And he wanted to follow the scent. He sniffed and sniffed but he couldn't figure out where it was coming from. Because it was everywhere. And then fall came and the scent was gone.—Oh yes, there's something I forgot: before that, from the corner of his eye your father saw a tiny thread floating in the air. It was silver, something fluffy and fuzzy was on one side. No, there were two threads, a bigger one and a very small one.

Two Members of the Chorus: (*follow him*) Someone from the outside, a stranger he had to marry. A girl from Radegund was not good enough for him. He had to marry someone from Hochburg. They think they are city people because from where they are at they can see Burghausen in Bavaria. That serves him right. He has to push a stroller now. And he's talking to himself. Now he's gone completely mad.

FRANZ: And winter came and I was slaving away with the wood, I'm telling you, Rosl. And it was cold and the frost almost bit off my fingers! And then spring came again, and one morning your father walked out of the house—and what happened? He passed out—plonk! And you know why, Rosl? The scent was back again. But so strong that your father fainted. He woke up, opened his eyes, there right in front of his nose were two golden flowers growing out of the grass. A tall flower and a very small one. Your father couldn't believe his eyes. And the scent of both, of the tall one and the small one, went through his nostrils directly to his heart. And it made him so happy. To this day the scent has been in my heart, Rosl. And all of a sudden my loneliness was gone. And you know who these two flowers are? Do you know it? It is you and your mother. (*He takes Rosl in his arms and hugs her.*)

11.

October 1940.

Franz (with Rosl on his lap) and Franziska (with Maridl on her lap, Loisi in her arm). He holds his official draft letter in his hands.

FRANZISKA: I told you to go to the municipality! They can issue a request on your behalf. You are the only man on the farm besides my father who occasionally helps us but can't do much anymore. Others are also exempt from military service.

FRANZ: I don't want them to petition on my behalf.

FRANZISKA: You don't want their child support money; you don't want their indemnity for hail damage…!

FRANZ: I don't want anything from them.

FRANZISKA: But they want something from us. We have to diligently deliver butter and cheese and oats and meat… the others are all cheating a bit to meet the quota but you…

FRANZ: Fani, I don't want to cheat.

FRANZISKA: Then take the money for child support! We're entitled to it!

FRANZ: I don't take anything and I don't give anything.

FRANZISKA: You're becoming more and more unpopular, do you know that? You can't send away children who collect for Winter Relief.

FRANZ: I don't want anything to do with the Hitler Youth.

FRANZISKA: That's for winter clothing for soldiers.

FRANZ: I know, you have to dress warm in order to shoot people. I don't give for that.

FRANZISKA: Is that Christian, Franz?

FRANZ: No poor and hungry person leaves this place with an empty backpack, you know that. But nothing for the swastika people. Get used to it.

FRANZISKA: What are you doing now? Please don't say you're not going there.

FRANZ: If not, would you say again that you don't like me?

FRANZISKA: No, Franz, I won't say that anymore. I promise. That was a sin. And it wasn't true. I will always love you.

FRANZ: (*strokes her cheek, then*) Everybody is in a delirium. In an ecstasy for victory. Even the most peaceful among them. Germany invades one country after the other. They call it a blitz. Holland, Belgium, France. All fell. (*He shakes his head.*) I don't shoot at people.

Franziska: You don't have to shoot at anybody now, Franz.

(*Takes the draft letter out of his hand, looks at it.*) At Enns, the Rifle Men Barracks. For basic training it says. For the motorcycle rifle troop. You can ride your motorbike. What's wrong about that? And then we will see. (*Looks at him.*) Please, dear husband. (*Franz kisses Rosl's head, contemplating.*)

12.

The Chorus (soldiers) marching, parading in formation up and down. Franz joins the group and marches with them.

FRANZISKA: (*reads her letter out loud*) Dearest husband, Plowing the field made me terribly angry; it was so bad that I was close to tears. Today I got a replacement for the plowing—my father came. He told me that Hias Erber is back home again because he had petitioned. My heart sank when I heard that. In God's name, I hope you won't stay very long. Rosl keeps asking about you when we go to bed. I'm not allowed to lock the front door. "Don't lock Father out," she says. And when we eat: "Save some for Father." Sometimes she cries because "Father is not coming." "Is he going to bring sausages?" Maridl asks.

FRANZ'S VOICE: Dearest spouse, I know that some of your work is harder now that I am not home. I believe you that your heart sinks sometimes. Dearest Fani, don't take it so hard. Seeing each other again will be such a delight. Sometimes I feel so happy because of you and the children that my eyes often are filled up with tears of joy.

FRANZISKA: Dearest husband, would you believe they arrested and imprisoned our venerable Reverend Karobath because of a sermon. We are all very sad and don't know who betrayed him. Because the head teacher doesn't go to church. I wanted to tell you we mowed all the grass except for the Grünschneider Meadow which still has a few truck loads of grass. I sold a couple of kilos of cabbage for 6 pennies. Marie got 64 kilos, Racheneder took 14 kilos, he paid 10 pennies. We have about 20 kilos left. When you come home again you can eat sweet cabbage again. Your mother says I should petition for you. What do you say?

FRANZ'S VOICE: Dearest spouse, I feel sorry about our venerable Reverend. He was the only one who remained forthright. Even I have become sheepish. Dear Fani, don't petition on my behalf. First we have to do infantry training and then the training to become motorcycle rifle men. I would have to start all over again if I deferred now. But I would welcome it very much once I'm done with my training, in about three months. How is the hay cutting coming? Did you grease and store the scythes?

Franziska and Franz face each other.

FRANZISKA: Rosi said yesterday I should get Father home with the motorbike. Thank you for for the chocolate and the sweets but you should have eaten them yourself. Mariandl said: "Father should send us a lot of chocolate." Lots of kisses from your little rascals.

FRANZ: Basic training is over now but nothing is going on. Can you go to the municipalities for the petition? And send greetings to the community leaders; tell them that I will keep fighting them even if they help me.

13.

Franziska, Mayor

FRANZISKA: I've been alone for almost six months now. I can't get all the work done by myself anymore, I just need him. The other farmers get time off or are exempt from military service.

MAYOR: Did he send you or you coming on your own?

FRANZISKA: He is finally sending me, I myself would have come a long time ago.

MAYOR: And I have been waiting for you for a long time. I know how hard you have been working. He and his false sense of pride. (*Hands her a paper.*) Here is the request on behalf of the municipality.

FRANZISKA: I have heard that things are expedited if the farmers' association supports it.

MAYOR: The farmers' association says that Jägerstätter doesn't want anything to do with us. That is why we do not want anything to do with him. Franz should personally deliver the request to the Commander; then it will work. He has already exempted a number of farmers from Radegund.

FRANZISKA: God bless you, Mayor.

MAYOR: I am doing this for you, Franziska, not for the bull-head. Had he become mayor he would have been exempted anyway. But now I am exempt.

FRANZISKA: Be glad.

MAYOR: I am. But I have to deal with them. And I have to raise my arm. And I have to try to protect all of you.

FRANZISKA: But you didn't protect the Reverend.

MAYOR: What can I do against the Gestapo? What? Why does he have to give a sermon like that?

MAYOR: (*after a pause*) The midwife wrote down his sermon. And she passed it on to the head teacher. And he informed the Gestapo.

FRANZISKA: I'm going to pass this on. Nobody will talk to him then. Nobody will give him food. Then he'll soon be finished.

MAYOR: Hopefully.

FRANZISKA: And we don't need the midwife either. We women will help each other. (*Wants to leave.*)

MAYOR: Wait.—When your husband comes home, you will have to make sure he keeps his mouth shut.

FRANZISKA: I won't be able to do that.

MAYOR: You will have to make sure of it; otherwise he will inevitably be arrested. (*Gets a torn letter out of his pocket.*) Do you know what this is? I got it from the woman at the post office because she was frightened when she saw the address. This is a letter from the head teacher to the Gestapo. It lists ten names. Your husband's name is among them—Sankt Radegund is far from everything, but it can hit us too, as you can see.

FRANZISKA: God bless you that you're with us. I'll bring the woman at the post office butter and bacon.

14.

Franz and Franziska facing each other.

FRANZ: We are on the way to the military training facility in Allensteig. I had to take over a couple of horses and a carriage. That was probably the major's doing again. Could you send me a bag of oats for my horses, they could need extra food.

FRANZISKA: Do you really have horses now? Don't get cocky now. Not everybody can afford them. But they are too wild for me, I prefer our pulling cattle. Unfortunately, I won't be able to send you any oats, I'll need it for our animals.

FRANZ: I hitched up the horses at 5am, didn't sleep, the major had me watch over the stable all night. 30 kilometers to Ybbs, a quite beautiful town on the Danube. Here they have a large psychiatric institution. Dear spouse, it is certainly true what happens to these poor people, as you told me once. The farmer we are staying with says that sad things had happened here. Good thing I don't have a motorbike or I would be unstoppable.

FRANZISKA: Our Loisi achieved something great today, she walked five steps but then she fell over. But she gets up again in no time! Soon we will need to sow and you're still not back. I hope I won't be leaving bare spots when I sow, because that is so important to me.

FRANZ: I have a feeling that you will have to sow oats without me this year. You should swap a few bags so you can grow different seeds. Or you could ask Schirk or Hirl, they have the best oats.

15.

Franziska hanging sheets. Head teacher approaches.

FRANZISKA: What do you want? Are you coming alone or with the Gestapo?

HEAD TEACHER: I am alone.

FRANZISKA: That's strange.

HEAD TEACHER: I asked to be transferred. It wasn't granted. I have to persevere as the Local Group Leader. That's what they say.

FRANZISKA: Poor man!

HEAD TEACHER: Nobody talks to me. Nobody looks at me. The children in school stubbornly refuse to look me in the eye; the whip is not helping either. They don't even scream when I hit them. With my food stamps I have to go to Ostermiething because Radegund doesn't have any bread, flour and noodles. The farmers used to give their children bacon and eggs and butter but those times are over.

FRANZISKA: Are you surprised?

HEAD TEACHER: Our Führer is sacred to me! National Socialism is sacred to me! And this war is also sacred to me!

FRANZISKA: Poor man.

HEAD TEACHER: Talk to the people of Radegund. Tell them that the Gestapo won't hear from me ever again. I swear.

FRANZISKA: I will talk to them.

HEAD TEACHER: Thank you. Heil Hitler. (*Starts to leave.*)

FRANZISKA: I can't guarantee it. Maybe you should volunteer. I mean to fight in the Holy War. (*The head teacher looks back sadly, departs.*)

16.

Franz arrives wearing civilian clothes.

FRANZISKA: Franz! (*Franziska runs towards him with the children. They hug and kiss each other. He hugs the children, throws one in the air, takes two in his arms.*)

FRANZ: Loisi! Maridl! My goodness, you have grown!

FRANZISKA: You didn't take off on your own?

FRANZ: No! They let me go. Indispensable! Indigestible! Children, I'm going to eat you up! Now, I'm sowing the oats after all. (*Looks around.*) Look, how everything is so green and blooming. (*Looks at her*). You're blooming too. How beautiful you are, Fani. (*Hugs her again.*)

FRANZISKA: (*cries*) I was yearning for you. It was terrible. As if they had cut off a part of me. (*Rosalia approaches, looks poorly.*)

FRANZ: Mother.

ROSALIA: (*gives him her hand*) My boy.

FRANZ: (*looks at her*) Are you alright?

ROSALIA: Couldn't be better. The farmer is back again.

FRANZISKA: Mother had cancer surgery. She didn't want me to write you about it. (*Franz is worried.*)

ROSALIA: Doesn't matter. I won't have any children anymore anyway. Don't need any. I have you, Franzl. You won't leave me, will you? (*Franz does not immediately answer.*) Did you hear me?

FRANZ: Mother. This is not the time to ask such a question. Our lives are in God's hand.

ROSALIA: No, not in God's hand.

FRANZISKA: (*to Franz*) You didn't tell me everything either, did you?

FRANZ: The major bullied me around a bit. I wasn't allowed to leave the barracks on Sundays, night watches, parading as punishment, forced marches in full gear, he in the car behind me…But he didn't break me. You can't break a farmer like that. Especially someone from the Innviertel.

FRANZISKA: But why? Why did he bully you around?

FRANZ: Because I went to Mass. (*Smiles.*) And because I never hit the target silhouette. (*Takes the backpack off his shoulders.*) But now the presents! Loisimaridlrosl, you won't believe it!

17.

War memorial service. Priest Fürthauer, Franz as Sacristan, Franziska with the children, Rosalia, Mayor, the Chorus.

PRIEST FÜRTHAUER: Brothers and sisters. Again we celebrate in proud sorrow a requiem for three young men from our village, whose bodily remains were buried by their comrades somewhere on the Russian front. I know it is painful, dear parents, that you will not be able to look into their faces to say farewell. But be comforted, your sons are in eternal blessedness; their glory will remain forever, because they have sacrificed themselves for their homeland and fatherland. They died a hero's death as brave soldiers—

FRANZ: (*interrupts*) They died in vain. In vain! Like sheep they were led to slaughter! For a criminal war!

CORYPHAEUS: Why are you denying our sons' honor?

CHORUS: Why are you denying our sons' honor? Why are you talking badly about our children?

FRANZ: It's honorable to live in peace and harmony. It's honorable to push the ploughshare in to the ground and to sow bread. Not to kill people in Russia and to be killed!

CORYPHAEUS: Why are you breaking our hearts, Jägerstätter?

CHORUS: Why are you breaking our hearts, Jägerstätter?

Why are you taking our proud sorrow from us?

FRANZ: Do you think it doesn't hurt me to lose my relatives, my friends and neighbors? I knew them all! These three too. We lived and worked with each other and on Sunday we went bowling and had a beer. I miss them as well!

PRIEST FÜRTHAUER: Jägerstätter! On the day the Russian Campaign began it became our war too, because it is a war against godless Bolshevism, which could destroy the entire world! Therefore, every Christian soldier is also God's soldier! Every Christian soldier, who falls on the field of glory, is also a martyr!

CHORUS: Every Christian solider is God's soldier! Every Christian soldier is a martyr. (*Franz departs in despair, pulls off his sacristan robe.*) Every Christian soldier is a martyr.

18.

Franz and Franziska. He has the conscription order. Long silence. Franziska is deeply troubled. Rosalia approaching with the priest and mayor. The Chorus in the background.

ROSALIA: Boy! You have to accept it. You can get the death penalty! The death penalty, do you know that?

MAYOR: As a soldier you have the chance to survive, Franz. And if you get killed, it's a quick death. But if they sentence you to death, you will have to wait and wait and wait. I've seen it thirty-four times, when I was in Linz. A relative of mine, a socialist, went insane until they finally hanged him.

PRIEST FÜRTHAUER: You don't have to aim at them if you don't want to kill anyone. By the way, you could do a lot of good on the front. You could take care of the wounded and dying comrades. You could protect civilians if sadistically inclined comrades want to commit unjust acts. As a good soldier you could consider yourself part of Christianity's lay apostolate.

Franz staring absentmindedly. Smiles sarcastically.

FRANZISKA: Franz! For the children and for me! What would we do without you?

CHORUS: (*approaches slowly*) For the children and for her.

MAYOR: I cannot believe it! He wants to abandon his family!

CHORUS: He wants to abandon his family.

MAYOR: You do not do that, Jägerstätter! A family father never abandons his family! Especially not a farmer! A scruffy bum maybe, a drunkard, a gambler, a sad dog!

CHORUS: A drunkard, a gambler, a sad dog.

MAYOR: But not you, Jägerstätter!

Franz becomes increasingly desperate.

PRIEST FÜRTHAUER: I should not be talking to you anymore; I am only here because of your family. Give to Caesar what is Caesar's.

CHORUS: Give to Caesar what is Caesar's.

PRIEST FÜRTHAUER: You must obey the power of authority, St. Paul says. You must fulfill your duty.

CHORUS: You must fulfill your duty.

PRIEST FÜRTHAUER: Thousands of theologians are out on the front! Do not tell me what a Catholic can and cannot do! You pigheaded man!

ROSALIA: Hide in the woods, there are others. I will bring you food. Maybe the war will soon be over anyway.

Mayor: I did not hear that, Rosalia. Desertion is the worst thing.

Chorus: Desertion is the worst thing.

Mayor: There is no greater shame than that.

Priest Fürthauer: (*to Rosalia*) They would pressure all of you. They have already taken entire families as hostages.— Franz! What you have in mind is suicide.

Chorus: Suicide. Suicide. Suicide.

Priest Fürthauer: And suicide is a deadly sin! You will rot in hell for that!

Rosalia: You need to join! I'm telling you as your mother. —I gave you your life; you don't have the right to throw it away. You owe me that.

Chorus: (*demanding*) Join! Join! Join!

Franz: (*crying out.*)

Franziska hugging Franz. Silence.

Franziska: Leave him alone. (*To Franz*) Do what you have to do. I stand by you.

19.

Franz and the Bishop of Linz. Franz kneels down, kissing the Bishop's ring, gets up, steps back, turns the hat in his hand.

BISHOP: You have religious issues with military service?

FRANZ: (*He has great respect for the Bishop.*) Yes, Excellency.

BISHOP: Are you a Jehovah's Witness?

FRANZ: No, I'm Catholic. And a Sacristan in our church.

BISHOP: But you like to talk to Jehovah's Witnesses, so we hear.

FRANZ: Those are relatives. A cousin of mine and his mother. For the most part.

BISHOP: And you have been influenced by them.

FRANZ: No, it's rather that I have tried for years to influence them. That they would return to the Catholic faith.

BISHOP: Jehovah's Witnesses refuse military service. In principle. I'm not really informed but a few hundred have been supposedly executed because of their conscientious objection.

Franz looks at the Bishop.

BISHOP: You have not been influenced by your cousin?

FRANZ: My cousin joined. He's fighting in Russia.

BISHOP: So your cousin joined even though the authorities of his sect dictated he was not to do it?

FRANZ: That is right.

BISHOP: And what about the Catholic Church? Does the Church forbid its believers to be a part of this war?

FRANZ: No, unfortunately, the Church doesn't.

BISHOP: Do not waste my time, Jägerstätter. Thirty seminarians and priests from my diocese have given their lives as Christian soldiers. And you want to get around it? As your spiritual leader I am saying to you: join! Are you going to obey me?

FRANZ: I must obey God. And Jesus Christ.

BISHOP: And you do not think I represent God's position. And Christ's? How dare you, farmer from the Innviertel!

FRANZ: (*agonized*) I only want a piece of advice, Excellency. It's been tormenting me.

BISHOP: What is your problem?

FRANZ: Your predecessor, Excellency, Bishop Gföllner, said in January 1933: "If according to Pope Pius XI's decree it is impossible to be a good Catholic and a true socialist, then it is equally impossible to be at once a good Catholic and a good National Socialist."

BISHOP: Spare me my predecessor's words, Jägerstätter. Firstly, that was 1933, we were not at war, and secondly, no one says a soldier has to be a true National Socialist. His task is to fight, that is all.

FRANZ: Since the beginning of the war I have been even more confused. Excellency, back then, the Holy Father in Rome said: "All Catholics should courageously fight with Christian love on whatever side they stand."

BISHOP: Yes, and? The Pope has to be strictly neutral. He is the head of all Catholics. In the entire world.

FRANZ: And so the Germans pray to God for victory, the French pray for victory and the Belgian, Dutch, and English Catholics, too. Who does God listen to? To the German Catholics apparently. Until now. Why?

BISHOP: You are splitting hairs, Jägerstätter. Do not pretend to be more naive than you are. We could not prevent the war. But now we are in a situation that concerns Bolshevism. And now we must—

FRANZ: (*interrupts*) I don't believe it! And neither do you! If you look at history, it's always the same: it's about greed! It's not about Bolshevism! It's about agriculture, metals, and oil resources! This war is unjust! Everybody talks about defending the fatherland! In 1938, we had a fatherland which we should have defended! Our fatherland Austria. What kind of defense is that when you invade foreign countries that don't owe us anything, only to rob and kill?

BISHOP: Is there an organization supporting you?

FRANZ: I stand alone! Completely alone! That's why I'm coming to you! National Socialism is godless, you know that! In our deanery, eight out of ten priests were arrested, you know that! Even our Pastor Karobath who was courageous enough to preach against those criminals!

BISHOP: Because of him the Gestapo searched all rectories in the diocese. Because of him, the Gauleiter threatened me with violent measures! Sometimes you just have to hold your tongue, Jägerstätter. This has nothing to do with being a coward. But with prudence. We cannot give them any opportunities.

FRANZ: I stand with the priests who would rather be imprisoned than shut up.

BISHOP: I cannot help you.

FRANZ: The red letters scrawled on your entrance door say: "Jew Christ! Rot in hell!"

BISHOP: Again? Do they not understand that Christ is God? He broke with Judaism. He has nothing to do with Judaism.

FRANZ: I beg you, Excellency. Whether a Jew is a Catholic or a Protestant, those criminals couldn't care less. All the Jews disappear. Where to? What's going on in the camps?— One has to stop them, Excellency. They take children out of orphanages and kill them. They are the Master Race and everybody else is subhuman. But we are all children of God. Doesn't the Church say that? Doesn't our faith say that?

BISHOP: Jägerstätter! You are not responsible for the acts of the ones in power. But you are responsible for your family. There is nothing you can do all by yourself; you must finally accept that.

FRANZ: Why isn't the Church doing anything? Why isn't it doing anything? Why doesn't the Holy Father speak out? Would they deport him to a camp?

BISHOP: That's enough.

FRANZ: The Pope in a concentration camp. Could you imagine that?

Bishop: Your time is up, Jägerstätter.

FRANZ: The head of a billion Catholics in a concentration camp. The Vatican's Head of State in a concentration camp? Would the Nazis dare to do it?

BISHOP: I am telling you, your time is up.

FRANZ: Am I allowed to do it?

BISHOP: It is up to you if you have a clear conscience.

FRANZ: I am asking you as my bishop: Am I allowed to do it?

BISHOP: I can tell you are thirsting for the passion of atonement, for martyrdom.

FRANZ: I am thirsting for justice, not martyrdom. I enjoy living! I am asking you a third time: am I allowed to do it?

BISHOP: If it is not coming from you but from a supernatural prophecy from above, then you are allowed to do it. But I doubt that.

FRANZ: May I ask for your blessing? I need a blessing.

The bishop is motionless. Franz turns away in disappointment and departs.

20.

February 1943.

Night. Franz is wrestling with himself. He is scared. He tears open his shirt, takes a butcher's knife, and as quick as a flash cuts a cross on his chest. He puts down the knife, buttons his shirt, puts on his jacket and coat. Franziska comes in; they hug each other for a long time. The farewell is heartbreaking. Franz pulls away. They look at each other. He makes the sign of the cross on his forehead, mouth, and chest. He kisses her, takes his hat and backpack, puts on his hat and leaves.

21.

Franz and an Austrian officer (Colonel) of the Wehrmacht. Behind Franz two soldiers with their weapons around their shoulders. They have brought him here and are now guarding him. A sergeant sitting at a typewriter takes minutes. In the background the Chorus as shadow army.

OFFICER: Jägerstätter, you are two days overdue. I had already issued a search for you. In Radegund they say you left in time. Where were you?

FRANZ: I got lost.

The sergeant typing.

OFFICER: What do you mean?

FRANZ: I got on the wrong train. Instead of going from Tittmoning to Enns, I went in the opposite direction to Munich.

OFFICER: Were you drunk or what?

FRANZ: No, Colonel. I just wanted to drag it out. I was simply scared.

OFFICER: Every soldier is scared. As long as you did not desert. (*To the two soldiers:*) Dismissed. (*The soldiers standing at attention, exit. The Colonel walks up to the sergeant, rips the paper from the typewriter. The sergeant grudgingly takes note of it. The officer crumples the paper and throws it in the wastebasket.*) Let's forget it, Jägerstätter.

FRANZ: But that's a misunderstanding, Colonel. I was afraid of my own decision.

OFFICER: I do not understand.

FRANZ: I'm sorry if this causes you any grief. You have been so kind to me.

OFFICER: What is going on, tell me!

FRANZ: I refuse to serve.

OFFICER: (*after a while*) No, you're not doing that to me.

FRANZ: I'm sorry, Colonel.

OFFICER: You know the consequence?

FRANZ: Yes, I do, Colonel.

OFFICER: Then you should have a good reason.

FRANZ: I'm a Catholic.

OFFICER: So am I. They are all Christians who serve in the field, more or less. (*Franz is tired having to argue all the time.*) You have something against the Nazis.

FRANZ: Yes, that's what it is.

OFFICER: (*points at his uniform*) You see this uniform here?

We are the Wehrmacht, we are the army. We are not a Nazi organization.

FRANZ: I see the imperial eagle with the sun wheel that is spinning towards hell.

OFFICER: He forced it on us. We still don't have anything to do with the Nazis.

FRANZ: But who is leading the war of the Nazis? It's the army.

OFFICER: Look, Jägerstätter. I fought for Austria during the First World War. On the side of the Germans. What followed? Austria as a dwarf state and Germany collapsing from reparations. This war was simply inevitable, it had to happen. It does not matter who is in charge of the government, the Nazis or a different party.

FRANZ: Unbelievable atrocities are being committed.

OFFICER: As in any war. Some people turn into beasts when they are officially permitted to kill.

FRANZ: Not only this permission, Colonel. Comrades from the Eastern front have told me that they are slaughtering civilians. And that's an order. They are slaughtering Jews. And that's an order.

OFFICER: It is March 2, 1943, Jägerstätter. And we know it is not looking good. And there are high officers in the

Wehrmacht who are concerned about our so-called Führer. Leave it to us, Jägerstätter. Your sacrifice would not change a thing. (*Franz is insecure and distraught. The officer sees the sergeant typing, walks up to him and rips the paper out of the typewriter again.*) Are you crazy or what? Are you going to denounce the company commander? I have the upper hand, sergeant. Do you want to trade the warm office with the frontline? (*The sergeant gives in, leans back.*) I truly wish you well, Jägerstätter. I admire your courage. (*Puts his hand on his shoulder.*) Would you report to the Medical Corps? To save comrades, to help people?

FRANZ: My priest said that too. But is it possible?

OFFICER: One cannot actually choose. But I will attend to it. (*Franz wrestles with himself.*) Take your objection back and no one will be informed about it. (*He looks at the sergeant.*) Right? (*The sergeant nods half-heartedly.*)

FRANZ: I already mentioned my objection to the guards outside the barracks. They recorded it.

OFFICER: (*stares at him in shock. The sergeant satisfied.*)

FRANZ: I wanted it behind me. I am sorry.

OFFICER: Idiot! I cannot believe it!—Guards! (*The two guards enter again.*)

OFFICER: You will be taken to the Wehrmacht prison in Linz where you will await trial. I know the commander there. Renounce your objection, please. Then we will do what we can to accommodate you in the Medical Corps. Agreed?

FRANZ: (*after a while*) Yes…alright. (*Distraught:*) No! I'm starting to give in again! I don't want to be a coward! I don't want to be lukewarm!

OFFICER: (*wearily and angry to the guards*) Take this man away!

22.

Wehrmacht prison in Linz. While we hear the contents of the following letters, Franz is being bullied around by the Chorus (a sergeant and four soldiers). They force him to put on a uniform, they want to put a rifle in his hand, he resists, they force him to, they force him to march to present arms, they hit him with the butt of the rifle, he falls, they kick him while on the ground, they hit him with the butt of the rifle again. Franz manages to take the rifle from one of the soldiers. He releases the safety catch, aims at the soldiers, they back away, he gets up, aims the rifle at himself, one pulls it out of his hand, they pound him unconscious. This action is done silently.

At the same time we see Franziska taking sheets from the clothes line.

FRANZ'S VOICE: Dearest spouse! Heartfelt greetings to you. Now I will have to stay here while I'm awaiting trial; for the time being I'm not doing badly. Should they ask you if you agreed with me that I shouldn't fight, tell them honestly how you felt about it.

FRANZISKA'S VOICE: Much beloved spouse! When I sent you letters two years ago, I was very melancholic, but at least I had the happy anticipation of seeing you again. But writing to you in your present situation saddens me terribly.

I had a little hope that you might change your mind on the way there.

Franz's voice: My beloved darling! I am letting you know that I have agreed to serve as a paramedic, because one can do good things there. But I was told that I will face punishment because of it.

Franziska's voice: Much beloved spouse! I wish you luck from the bottom of my heart for your decision and I look forward to seeing you again if it's God's will. When we plant oats you should be able to return and to rake, to plant potatoes and do all the big and difficult tasks. Greetings from your three girls. Maridl says she's going to help you catch Russians so that you can come home earlier.

Franz's voice: Most beloved spouse! I have a request of you: could you put a few edelweiss flowers in your next letter? It's for a young man from Lorraine, a conscientious objector, who was sentenced to death. He would want to send his beloved an Edelweiss because she loves flowers.

Franziska's voice: Dearest Husband! Our relatives keep telling me I should come visit you but the farewell is always so heartbreaking for both of us, isn't it?

Franz's voice: I would not recommend visiting me at this point. They would only allow 15 minutes. Dearest spouse, today it was seven years ago we promised each other love and loyalty before God. Your new husband is sending his greetings to you. They say that man renews himself every seven years. So as of today you have a new husband. I want to advise you to buy a few scythes so that cutting the grass will at least be easier.

FRANZISKA'S VOICE: Last night the Tiefenthaler cow gave birth, of course without our help. The baby is a lively calf. Dearest! Our orchard is going to be wonderful again this year. The pear and plum trees are standing in full bloom, and the apple trees are already beginning to blossom. It is so beautiful going for a walk with the children; too bad that you can't be home. While off-duty, Gänshanger cut off all four of his fingers while he was cutting food for the animals. Of course, the police came by because of self-mutilation.

The Chorus (soldiers) withdrawing. Two soldiers pull Franz up and handcuff him.

23.

Wehrmacht prison in Berlin-Tegel. Franz, handcuffed, being led to his prison cell by two soldiers. Prison guards, called "jailers" ("Schliesser"), who are known for their brutality, take over. They rip off Franz's uniform coat. One guard hands him a tin bowl, another guard scoops a thin cabbage soup from a pot with a ladle. Franz holds up his bowl; the guard pours the hot soup over his hands, Franz drops to his knees. Again the guard scoops soup from the pot, while another guard clubs Franz on his head. Franz holds up his bowl again and the guard pours the hot steaming soup over his hands once again. This action is done silently.

FRANZ'S VOICE: (*during the torture scene*) My beloved darling! I arrived safely at on May 4th 11pm in Berlin. The departure from Linz was very surprising. Don't worry about me. I have a very small, nice chamber alone. Unfortunately, we're only allowed to write one letter per month. If I had known that I had to leave Linz without being tried, I would have asked you to visit me, because it's too far for you to Berlin. If it is God's will, we will see each other again in this world and if not then in a different world where visiting hours will be a bit longer. Heartfelt greetings from your loving husband. My dear children, don't forget your father and pray for him. Be blessed in the protection of the heavenly mother.

24.

Prison cell in Berlin-Tegel. Franz and his assigned counsel, Friedrich Feldmann (with his briefcase). He is wearing a Wehrmacht officer's uniform (captain).

FELDMANN: (*takes off his cap, shakes Franz's hand*) Dr. Feldmann, I am your assigned counsel.

FRANZ: God's greeting!

FELDMANN: Who is greeting me? (*Franz doesn't understand.*) I'm just joking. I know these types of greetings from the Tyrol. Went skiing there. Do you know what they say around here when you say "Hail Hitler?" "Why don't you hail him?" (*Laughs. Franz doesn't know how to react. Feldmann searches his briefcase, looks for the file.*) No worries, this is the Wehrmacht, not the Gestapo. And you won't be tried by a people's court. That's where you would lose heart while Judge Freisler would rip you to shreds. There every one is already sentenced to death. Head off or hanging. On a butcher's hook. With us, everyone has a chance. Especially someone like you. An idealist—(*Finds the file.*) Here it is. (*Looks at the file, opens it.*) Jägerstätter, Franz. Roman Catholic. Conscientious objector because of his faith.—Beats me what you Austrians find in your Catholicism. Protestantism is the religion of men.— Ouch! (*Laughs.*) Braunau county! Disadvantageous area for a conscientious objector. (*Puts paper down and fountain pen.*) You sign this and the thing is settled.

FRANZ: What is that?

FELDMANN: You recant your objection.

FRANZ: And I can be a paramedic?

FELDMANN: (*looks at him astounded, looks at the file*) That is what it actually says. You volunteered for the Medical Corps in Linz. But it doesn't work in that way. No soldier can pick his unit.

FRANZ: My commander in Linz promised it—somehow.

FELDMANN: Nothing happens "somehow" in the military, my dear Jägerstätter. Of course, time and again there are cases that a soldier, who has connections, who knows someone, may join the unit he desires. But not if he's a conscientious objector. Had you joined properly, yes, maybe your commander could have possibly helped you. (*Franz is stunned.*) Come on now, Jägerstätter, you sign this and the thing is settled.

FRANZ: What does settled mean?

FELDMANN: You keep your head.

FRANZ: And then?

FELDMANN: The usual in such a case. Punishment battalion.

(*Franz as if struck by lightning.*)

FELDMANN: Think about it. We have time. (*Looks at the file.*) The trial before the military court is scheduled for July 6.

FRANZ: Why did they bring me to Berlin? In Linz they also have a military court. People are sentenced to death and executed there as well.

FELDMANN: Look, Jägerstätter. Most of the accused are deserters. They are killed quickly wherever they are. No use for cowards in times of war. But conscientious objectors are a more complicated matter. The Wehrmacht honors courage. And it is courageous if someone has himself beheaded out of conviction. If he looks death in the eye. We would like these people out on the front lines. We desperately need these people out on the front lines. Especially now. And that's why you are here in Berlin. We want to convince you not to die a meaningless death, Jägerstätter. (*Franz quiet.*) What is it one fights for in a war?

FRANZ: For one's country?

FELDMANN: Your country is Austria. (*Looks at the file.*) You are making a point about that. What is it one fights for, Jägerstätter?

FRANZ: For an ideology?

FELDMANN: Ideology is crap.

FRANZ: For freedom?

FELDMANN: Revolutionaries fight for freedom. (*Franz is clueless.*) You fight for your comrade. Only for the comrade, the one next to you in the trench, the one who dashes forward next to you. Your comrade watches out for you and you watch out for your comrade. He gives you his bread and you give him yours. You share the last cigarette. And when he's wounded you pull him out of the fire. At the risk of your own life. That is a good, honorable war. (*Franz is apprehensive.*) Think about it. We need you. Don't force us to chop your head off. That would hurt us.

Feldmann packs his things, puts a pack of cigarettes with matches on the table, puts on his cap, salutes Franz, leaves. Franz who had given up smoking some time ago, takes a cigarette and after a while, lights and smokes it.

25.

Franz sits as before. In front of him there is a letter from Franziska, but he is looking at a picture in his hand.

FRANZISKA'S VOICE: My beloved darling! The good news: the head teacher was transferred. The bad news: Sankt Radegund is not its own township anymore. We are now considered part of Ostermiething, that's where some people with power live. They swore to keep a close eye on us. As you can see I have a surprise for you today. Lini Schirk took pictures of your three favorites and I got them this week. Can you believe how big they have gotten, even Loisi, do you still recognize her? (*We see the picture that was sent in the letter projected in the background. The three girls hold a banner that says "Dear father, come soon." Franz stares at the picture in his hand which clearly breaks his heart. He gets up, walks around, groans loudly.*) It looks as if Loisi has so many eggs in her basket that she can't carry it anymore. They got the baskets from Rosi Zauner; they had a lot of fun with them. Your girls want me to tell you that they have collected a lot of kisses and they want you to come soon so you can have them. Loisi says that when you return she won't be sleeping next to me; only next to her father all of the time; I would be fine with that as long as you could come home. For your upcoming name day we wish you all the best, especially health. I'm always thinking of you. Your loving spouse, Fani.

26.

Franz (with a rosary in his hand) and Feldmann.

FELDMANN: The medical officer's report came in. He says you are absolutely normal; your mental capacity is beyond reproach.

FRANZ: Thanks, that's encouraging. I have often been called abnormal and a lunatic.

FELDMAN: It wouldn't have worked out anyway. You know what happens to the mentally ill these days. One hears bad things. A lethal injection is salvation in comparison.—So, Herr Jägerstätter? Have you thought about it?

FRANZ: Yes, for nights. You have really tempted me, Dr. Feldmann. Comradery is something to be treasured. Belonging to a community that sticks together, going through thick and thin together, that's just wonderful. I was cut off from everybody. From my family, my village, my congregation. It's not nice to be alone and completely misunderstood. My wife still stands by me, she's the only one, but in her heart of hearts she wants me to give in. Who can blame her because she loves and needs me. We used to be the most beautiful couple in the village, we still are. As it was on the first day. And we have three sweet girls, look. (*Franz shows Feldmann the picture, he looks at it.*)

FELDMANN: What kind of a man are you? "Dear father, come soon." (*Shows him the picture.*) What a stubborn man you are. Can you reconcile that with your Christian faith?

FRANZ: I have to obey God more than men.

FELDMANN: Martyr, right? "O Sacred Head, Now Wounded" The blood-drenched Christ on the cross. In every living room. A hanged man. A tortured one. A dead man.

FRANZ: He is risen.

FELDMAN: You Catholics are masochists. That's also Hitler's problem. He hates the Catholics but yet he is one himself. Some of the cruelest butchers, including him, come from Catholic Austria. You know that, Jägerstätter? You are all worshipping death.

FRANZ: I am not! That's not me! I believe in eternal life! This here on earth is just a transition!

FELDMANN: Nonsense! (*Rips the rosary out of his hand, throws it on the ground.*) That's as nonsensical as Valhalla! Blood sacrifices for the people, blood sacrifices for God! One and the same thing! This life is certain. Everything else is speculation, superstition. Here, in this world we have to persist, hold our own. We have to serve the state and (*shows him the picture*) our family! (*Franz wrestles with himself.*) I need a decision from you. Do you recant or not?

FRANZ: (*after a while*) No. I cannot. Not for those criminals. And now even punishment battalion. Galvanizing the bandit war, right? Isn't that what you call it? I call them partisan freedom fighters. And since we won't catch them because they are in the woods and mountains where they know their way, I will have to burn down their villages and their families. I know too much, I have been well informed, Dr. Feldmann. Not everyone keeps quiet, when they are on furlough.

FELDMANN: That's the end then, Jägerstätter. Very unfortunate (*Leaves.*)

27.

Franziska and Theresia, who is eating potatoes with boiled cabbage out of a tin bowl. Franziska watches her.

THERESIA: My farmer kicked me out. Can't pay me anymore, he says. Gets two women from Ukraine, forced laborers. They don't cost him anything. But the truth is he kicked me out because I was for Hitler. And his sons were killed for Hitler.

FRANZISKA: Now you're not for Hitler anymore, are you?

THERESIA: No.

FRANZISKA: And why not?

THERESIA: Because he's losing the war. He is a little man from Braunau, after all.

FRANZISKA: How's Hilde doing?

THERESIA: Hilde's in an orphanage.

FRANZISKA: In an orphanage? How come?

THERESIA: Because my mother died. And I will have to report to the Reich Labor Service.

FRANZISKA: Bring her to me! Please, bring her to me.

THERESIA: You're not getting my child. Not you.—You

didn't just take away my Franz. You sent him to death. Or isn't it true that he's waiting for his execution in Berlin?

Franziska: That was his decision!

Theresia: That was your decision, you, the "proper" girl, bigot, hypocrite! You got him into it!

Franziska: You're not going to talk to me that way.

Theresia: That's what they all say. And I just wanted to tell it to your face. (*Puts the plate down loudly, wipes her mouth in her sleeve.*) Thanks a lot for dinner. (*Gets up, begins to leave, turns around.*) If Franz's mother keeps telling everybody that he's not Hilde's father and that I sleep with everyone then I'm going to get her. She'll soon find out. Tell her that. (*Departs. Franziska collapses and sobs.*)

28.

Two guards and Franz. One is holding a cross and spits on it. They want to force Franz to spit on it as well. He refuses, they hit him with clubs, he rips the cross out of the guard's hand, kisses it, they knock him on the ground. This action is done silently.

FELDMANN'S VOICE: (*over the action*) Dear Reverend Fürthauer, Today, on July 6, 1943, Jägerstätter was sentenced to death by the Reich Court Martial in Berlin for subversion of the war effort. Even though I was able to persuade the judge before the trial to speak to my client in order to convince him to recant, your parishioner remained unreasonable. All that remained was the death sentence. But there is one final possibility as the sentence has not been confirmed. Reich's councilor of the court-martial Loeben, who was in charge of the trial, assured me that the confirmation and execution of the sentence will be delayed, if Frau Jägerstätter agrees to travel to Berlin in order to change her spouse's mind. With German greetings, Dr. Feldmann.

29.

Visitor's room, Prison Berlin-Tegel. Franziska (with back-pack) and priest Fürthauer are waiting. Franz, in handcuffs behind his back, is brought in by two guards (members of the Chorus). Franz sees Franziska and freezes. A soldier hits the butt of his gun into Franz's back, Franz stumbles and falls at Franziska's feet.

FRANZISKA: Franz!

She helps him get up. He looks at her stunned. Then his face is filled with joy.

FRANZ: That I would see you one last time...!

She embraces him. He can't embrace her because of the handcuffs. A soldier separates them, gestures to them to keep a distance from each other.

FRANZISKA: I brought you some red currant cake.

She wants to get the cake out of her backpack; a soldier gestures not to do it. Franz glowering; he can't believe it.

PRIEST FÜRTHAUER: Franz!

FRANZ: At first I thought you were an angel.

PRIEST FÜRTHAUER: Franz!

FRANZ: You came such a long way!

FRANZISKA: How are you?

Franz walks up to her, is pulled back.

FRANZISKA: The children are sending their greetings. You should finally come home and tell them stories.

PRIEST FÜRTHAUER: Franz, we don't have much time left.

Only now, Franz notices the priest.

FRANZ: Dear Reverend, God bless you, I will never forget that.

FRANZISKA: Why didn't you write me that they had sentenced you?

FRANZ: I wanted to wait until it was confirmed. I would have never thought I would see you again in this world. You look completely exhausted. My beloved!

Walks up to her, puts his head on her shoulder. She embraces him. The soldiers brutally pull him back, he falls. Franziska can't stand it, cries out, and can't suppress her crying. Franz ignores the brutality, gets up, his gaze remains on Franziska.

PRIEST FÜRTHAUER: Franz! We have come to save your life!

Franz smiling only at Franziska. The priest walks up to him, shakes him.

PRIEST FÜRTHAUER: Listen to me, please! They are giving you a chance, the final chance, to recant your objection.

FRANZ: (*looks at Franziska, smiling*) I am not here anymore.

PRIEST FÜRTHAUER: You are breaking the Fourth Commandment, do you know that? You are breaking the Fourth Commandment!

FRANZ: (*looks at Franziska*) "Honor your father and your mother, that your days may be long in the land which the Lord your God gives you."

PRIEST FÜRTHAUER: That also means that the parents should honor their children.—Look at me when I'm talking to you! (*Moves Franz's head towards him.*) As a father you have to honor your children and must not abandon them! And the Fourth Commandment also means that a believer has to honor his spiritual leader; he has to obey his priest. And it includes the relationship between the citizen and the state. The citizen has to obey the authority of the state. The Fourth Commandment includes all that. And you are breaking it! Three times! That means you are a terrible sinner!

FRANZ: "Whoever loves father or mother more than me is not worthy of me."

FRANZISKA: (*crying*) You're cruel!

PRIEST FÜRTHAUER: Be reasonable, Franz, be reasonable!

Feldmann enters, distraught.

FELDMANN: Jägerstätter! Colonel Loeben shot himself last night, the Reich's councilor of the court-martial. Next to his head was your note. In it, you thanked him for his understanding and patience but that he should go ahead and confirm the sentence as you wouldn't change your mind under any circumstances. And in his farewell letter he says he did not want to continue as the executioner of people who follow their conscience.

FRANZ: The Lord may accept him in paradise.

FELDMANN: I have met the judges, Jägerstätter. If you recant your objection, they will waive the punishment battalion.

FRANZ: (*shouting in desperation*) Stop torturing me! I want it to be over! God in heaven! (*Franziska embraces him.*) Forgive me, Fani.

The soldiers walk up to them and try to separate them. Franziska clings to him, the soldiers pull her away, she falls to the ground, the soldiers drag Franz away.

30.

FRANZ'S VOICE: My dearest spouse! And all my beloved ones! I am writing with my hands chained, but it's still better than having my will chained. It has been four weeks since the last time we saw each other in this world. Today, it is the 9th of August, early in the morning, we had to get dressed quickly, the truck was already waiting and together with fifteen other prisoners who were sentenced to death we went to Brandenburg. Not before noon I was told that the sentence had been confirmed on July 14 and that I would be executed today at 4pm. Dearest spouse and mother, it has not been possible for me to free you from the pain you are suffering because of me. My heartfelt thanks for everything you have done in my life for all your love and sacrifices you have given for me. Forgive everything I have done to you and when I have offended you. And please ask all people in Radegund, whom I offended, for forgiveness. I don't think badly about people who act differently. It is better to pray for everyone because God wants them to find salvation. You shall love your God and your neighbor like yourself. There is no other commandment greater than these. Rosl, Maridl, Loisi, I love you very much and embrace you. I wanted to return to you so badly, but our Heavenly Father had other plans. Hildegard, my big girl, and you, Theresia, her mother, I am so glad to have known you. Forgive me, both of you, if possible. I am sending my greetings to you before my last journey. Your spouse, son, father, son-in-law and brother-in-law. Mary with Child give us your blessing.

In the meantime, Franziska working with a sickle in a grain field, cutting ears, bundles and binds them, puts them on wooden poles with hooks in order to dry them. Silence after Franz's last words. One hears the guillotine as it falls and cuts off Franz's head. Franziska reaches high and feels cut in half by the guillotine herself.

FRANZISKA: (*quietly*) Franz? (*She collapses. The bishop appears.*)

BISHOP: I deem all those ideal Catholic young men, theologians, priests, and fathers as the greater heroes who in heroic fulfillment of their duties and deeply Christian conviction to do God's will fought and fell. Or are the Jehovah's Witnesses and Adventists who rather died in camps than in the field, the greater heroes? I respect an innocent and lost conscience; God will honor that too. For pedagogical reasons, the examples of the fighting heroes, are the better models; those who definitely followed the right conscience by being consistent in their actions. For that reason, I do not find it opportune to report about Franz Jägerstätter's fate in the church newspaper. That would only antagonize thousands of believers who have returned to the bosom of the Church and it would burden people's peace of mind. Linz, February 27, 1946.

Franziska getting up. Franz approaches her. They look at each other. Franz smiles at her, she smiles too; he starts cutting and bundling grains. She does the same. Together they bring in the harvest. The Head Teacher appears.

Head Teacher: Dear Frau Jägerstätter! According to the Welfare Law for Victims, a victim is a person who fought with guns, word or deed against the goals and ideas of National Socialism and for a free and democratic Austria. As stated by the report of the police battalion Ostermiething, dated March 21, 1948, your spouse, Franz Jägerstätter, was an opponent of National Socialism, but his actions were not carried out in order to create a free and democratic Austria, as defined by paragraph 1 of the Welfare Law for Victims of 1947. He was a known melancholic and when drafted he stated that he would not fight for Hitler. His conviction was not steeped in defending a free Austria against National Socialism but rather in his religious world view. For this reason, your petition for support for widows and orphans at the Braunau municipality was rejected. Linz, August 10, 1948.

Franz and Franziska turning towards each other, they look at each other happily.

31.

For about 10 seconds, scenes of recent wars and of cruelty are projected. The sound deafeningly loud. Then silence.

CHORUS: Blessed Franz Jägerstätter, pray for us.

Blessed Franz Jägerstätter, pray for us.

Blessed Franz Jägerstätter, pray for us.

THE END

Franz Jägerstätter after his return from Eisenerz.

Franz Jägerstätter doing military training, winter 1940.

Franz Jägerstätter with his family.

Easter 1943, Rosalia, Maria and Aloisia. The banner reads "Dear father, come soon!"

Franziska Jägerstätter

Franz Jägerstätter

CONTRIBUTORS

FELIX MITTERER (*1948) is one of Austria's most celebrated contemporary authors. He has written numerous award-winning plays, radio plays, and TV scripts. The ORF, Austria's Public Broadcasting Cooperation, began producing his dramatized texts in 1970. Since the publication of his first play, *Kein Platz für Idioten* (*No Place for Idiots*) in 1977, Mitterer has been regarded as one of the leading Austrian playwrights. His many literary awards include the Ernst Toller Prize, the Adolf Grimme Prize, and most recently the Ödön von Horvath Prize. His dramatic works and film scripts are particularly well known for their critique of Austrian politics and society. His *Piefke Saga* (1988/1989) was a highly controversial and enormously successful television mini-series that critically and satirically illuminated the complex relationship between Austrians and Germans. Mitterer has also written twelve scripts for the well-known *Tatort* crime show which is co-produced by Austrian, German, and Swiss public television stations. Among his most successful plays for theater are *Die Kinder des Teufels* (*Children of the Devil*), *In der Löwengrube* (*In the Lion's Den*), and *Sibirien* (*Siberia*). After living in Ireland for fifteen years, Mitterer returned to Austria in 2011.

GREGOR THUSWALDNER is Professor of German and Linguistics at Gordon College in Wenham, Massachusetts and Co-Founder and Academic Director of The Salzburg

Institute of Religion, Culture and the Arts, an independent non-profit organization. A native of Salzburg, Austria, he studied German and English at the University of Salzburg, Bowling Green State University, the University of Vienna (Mag. phil.) and received his Ph.D. in Germanic Languages from the University of North Carolina at Chapel Hill. He has published articles and book chapters on Christoph Martin Wieland, Thomas Bernhard, Michael Haneke, Michael Scharang, Stanley Hauerwas, literary theory, linguistics, German and Austrian literature, culture, politics, and religion. His articles and book reviews have also appeared in German, Austrian, and American newspapers.

He is a co-editor of the essay collections *Der untote Gott: Religion und Ästhetik in deutscher und österreichischer Literatur des 20. Jahrhunderts (2007)* and *Making Sacrifices: Visions of Sacrifice in American and European Cultures* (2015). In 2008, he edited the essay collection *Derrida und danach? Literaturtheoretische Diskurse der Gegenwart.* Dr. Thuswaldner's monograph entitled "Morbus Austriacus"— Thomas Bernhard's *Österreichkritik* appeared in 2011. He is currently working on a monograph on Stefan Zweig.

ROBERT DASSANOWSKY is Professor of German and Film, and director of the Film Studies Program at the University of Colorado, Colorado Springs, and works as an independent film producer. His research centers on Central European and American cinema and on twentieth century Austrian and German literature and culture, and he has written for stage and television. A past president of the

Austrian Studies Association, Dr. Dassanowsky currently serves on the advisory board of the Salzburg Institute of Religion, Culture and the Arts, and on the editorial boards of the Journal of Austrian Studies, Colloquia Germanica, and Ariadne Press. He is a member of the Austrian and the European Film Academies, PEN USA and PEN Austria, and is a Fellow of the Royal Historical Society (UK). He was named the 2004 Carnegie Foundation/CASE U.S. Professor of the Year for Colorado, received the CU Thomas Jefferson Award in 2015, and presented the 2015 Annual Botstiber Institute for Austrian-American Studies Lecture. His books include *Austrian Cinema: A History* (2005), *New Austrian Cinema*, co-ed. with Oliver C. Speck (2011), *The Nameable and the Unnameable: Hugo von Hofmannsthal's* Der Schwierige *Revisited*, co-ed. (2011), *Quentin Tarantino's Inglourious Basterds: A Manipulation of Metafilm*, ed. (2012), *World Film Locations: Vienna*, ed. (2012), and the forthcoming *Screening Transcendence: Film under Austrofascism and the Hollywood Hope 1933-38*.

GÜNTER BISCHOF is a native of Austria and graduate of the Universities of Innsbruck, New Orleans, and Harvard (PhD '89). He is a University Research Professor of History, the Marshall Plan Professor and Director of CenterAustria: The Austrian Marshall Plan Center for European Studies at the University of New Orleans; he served as a visiting professor at the Universities of Munich, Innsbruck, Salzburg, Vienna, Louisiana State University-Baton Rouge, Liberal Arts University in Moscow, and the Economics

Universities of Vienna and Prague, as well as Hebrew University in Jerusalem; he is the author and editor of many books. With UNO Press he is publishing the series *Contemporary Austrian Studies* (24 vols) and *Studies in Central European History, Culture & Literature* (2 vols).